Global Inequality, Global Poverty, and Poverty Reduction in the Least Developed Countries

New Edition

JClaude Germain, Ph.D.

Table of Contents

List of Tables

List of Figures

About the Author

JClaude Germain is a Ph.D. economist with a specialization in International Economics and Development Economics. He is a Harvard-educated professional in International Development and Environmental Policy and Economic Growth.

He is the author of *Trade Liberalization and Globalization; The Impact of Corruption on Growth and Development; Global Inequality, Global Poverty and Poverty Reduction in the Least Developed Countries,* and several articles on global issues.

Dr. Germain had worked in the international community for over 14 years and taught economics for 12 years at the university level.
The author can be contacted at
drjcgermain@gmail.com

Dedication

In memory of my late
Father and Mother
Godfather and Godmother
Sister Servela

Acronyms

1	FAO	Food & Agriculture Organization of the United Nations
2	GDP	Gross Domestic Product
3	GNI	Gross National Income
4	HAI	Human Assets Index
5	HDI	Human Development Index
6	HIPCs	Heavily Indebted Poor Countries
7	IMF	International Monetary Fund
8	LDC	Least Developed Country
9	LIC	Low-income Country
10	MeRONS	Measurable Result-Oriented National Strategy

11	MPI	Migration Policy Institute
12	MDRI	Multilateral Debt Reduction Initiative
13	ODC	Other Developing Country
14	ODI	Overseas Development Institute
15	OECD	Organization for Cooperation and Economic Development
16	PPE	Pro-poor Public Expenditure
17	PPP	Purchasing Power Parity
18	PRS	Poverty Reduction Strategy (PRS) Initiative
19	PRSPs	Poverty Reduction Strategy Papers
20	SDRs	Special Drawing Rights
21	UN	United Nations
22	UNCTAD	United Nations Conference on Trade and Development

23	UNDP	United Nations Development Programme
24	UNFPA	United Nations Population Fund
25	UNIRSD	United Nations Institute for Research and Development
26	UNU	United Nations University
27	USDA	United States Department of Agriculture
28	WEF	World Economic Forum
29	WHO	World Health Organization
30	WIDER	World Institute for Development and Economics Research
31	WIR	World Inequality Report

Definition of Terms

Brain Drain - The emigration of highly educated and skilled professionals and technicians from their home country to another country (most commonly from developing to developed countries).
Ceteris Paribus Latin for "other things remaining equal."

Concessional Terms - Terms of credit that are more favorable to the borrower than those available through standard financial markets.

Economic Growth - A persistent increase in per capita aggregate output and in the aggregate physical capital per worker in an economy.

Income Inequality - The disproportionate distribution of total national income among households.

GDP Per Capita - A country's gross domestic product divided by its population.

Global GDP - The total market value of all goods and services produced around the world during a specific period of time, usually a year. In other words, it is the combined gross national income of all countries in the world.

NGO - Non-Governmental Organization

Poverty - The situation of people who cannot afford an adequate standard of living. Poverty can be viewed as an absolute or as a relative concept.

Poverty Line - An income level that is just sufficient to avoid less than adequate consumption.

Poverty Trap - A situation in which poverty outcomes reinforce themselves, acting as causes of poverty.

Predatory Dumping - The selling of an exported product on a foreign market at less than market value to beat the local competition, and once the competition is eliminated, the price generally increases.

Predatory Pricing - The policy of setting a price for a product at less than market value to drive out competition and/or deter new entrants to the market.

Purchasing Power Parity - The nominal exchange rate at which a given basket of goods and services would cost the same amount in each country in the long run.

Rent Seeking – "Spending time and money not on the production of real goods and services, but rather on trying to get the government to change the rules so as to make one's business more profitable". In economics, rent-seeking occurs when an individual, organization, or business tries to manipulate the economic and/or legal system to make money.

Remittance - A transfer of money by a foreign worker to individuals in his or her home country.

Special Drawing Rights - A form of the international financial asset created by the International Monetary Fund (IMF). SDRs are simply a form of credit extended to IMF members; they do not represent actual money and are defined as "a weighted average of various convertible currencies."

Wealth Inequality - The disproportionate distribution of total wealth in an economy.

Preface

As the global community has pledged to "reduce poverty and promote shared prosperity" across the globe, I published a study titled *Poverty Reduction in the Least Developed Countries* (LDCs).

I have decided to expand and re-publish the study under a new title: *Global Inequality, Global Poverty, and Poverty Reduction in the Least Developed Countries.* The rationale for re-publishing the study under a new title is that in the first publication, I directly delved into the analysis of poverty reduction without examining the issues of global inequality and global poverty, whereas there has been a consensus that "policy cannot successfully target poverty reduction…without addressing income inequalities". The sections on global inequality and global poverty will serve as a backdrop to the section on "*Poverty Reduction in the Least Developed Countries.*"

This study uses a critical, analytical and informative approach to stimulate new conversations that might be conducive to the implementation of policies that are more effective, targeted, and results-oriented. This represents an alternative approach to the consideration of the issues in this study, which is in search of concrete solutions to the enduring problems being examined. This *alternative* approach questions the events and what others have said and done.

Keywords: Economic inequality; global poverty; poverty reduction; developing countries; least developed countries; international institutions; United Nations; global economy.

Introduction

Economic inequality within and across countries has been on the rise. It has become a predominant global issue in recent decades because the economic gaps between the rich and the poor have widened across the globe. It is estimated that the world's richest 1 percent own approximately 50 percent of the world's wealth. This high level of economic disparity is usually manifested in high levels of poverty in some groups of individuals and countries.

Poverty exists in all countries - both developed and developing – but its level of severity varies between and within countries, depending on several factors that this study will examine. Global poverty is considered one of the worst problems facing the world today.

"The poorest in the world are often hungry, have much less access to education, regularly have no light, and suffer from much poorer health" (Roser & Ortiz-Ospina, 2013).

Although poverty is a global phenomenon, it is more acute and concentrated among a group of countries designated by the United Nations as **Least Developed Countries (LDCs)**. This study will focus on this group.

This paper is structured as follows: *Part one* (1) of the study will examine the issue of global economic inequality; its causes and consequences; and some of the proposed solutions to the problem; *Part two* (2) will consider the state of poverty at the global level; its causes and consequences; and some of the proposed solutions to remedy the situation; *Part three* (3) will provide information on some features of the LDCs and analyze some of the issues pertaining to this group of countries; consider the assistance granted to the LDCs; and examine the obstacles to their graduation. And the last chapter will conclude the study.

Part One: Global Economic Inequality

Chapter One:
Economic Inequality

T his section will explain the concept of economic inequality, examine its causes and consequences and analyze some potential solutions, but its principal purpose is to set a linkage between inequality and poverty, which will lead us to the main topic of this study - *Poverty Reduction in the Least Developed Countries* as a group.

In an attempt to find ways to stop and decrease growing income and wealth inequalities and increase economic opportunities for those in lower and middle classes, and the least developed countries, economists, policymakers, politicians, and international institutions have been debating the issue in recent years. Although they have not been able to agree on or find solutions to these enduring problems, they agree on the importance of narrowing economic disparities to pre-empt further socio-economic and political upheavals.

Although economic inequality is related to various characteristics of people's positions within the economic distribution, this study focuses on the two principal components – income and wealth. That said, let us first address the two concepts to dispel any confusion that might arise in the mind of some readers.

1.1 Income and Wealth

Income usually refers to money, goods, or services from an activity. It may be a return on the factors of production in the form of salary, rent, interest, or profit, or it may be a transfer payment such as a pension or unemployment. People also talk about non-monetary income – such as the benefit a company or an individual derives from the possession of assets. They also talk about earned incomes and unearned incomes. For the purpose of this study, *income is what people earn every year*.

Income Inequality usually refers to differences and disparity in income among individuals or families, or groups, or among areas or countries. In other words, it is an uneven distribution of total national income among a population, households, or countries.

Wealth refers to "the total value of a person's or a country's assets, both tangible and intangible." It may be held in the forms of money, shares in companies, land, debt instruments (bonds), buildings or assets (and other physical properties with liquidity value), intellectual property, and works of art. Inheritance is a component of wealth, which in part explains the wide gap between individuals and countries in terms of wealth. In short, *wealth is people's accumulated fortune.*

Wealth Inequality refers to the uneven distribution of assets among groups of people or countries.

How is wealth inequality measured?

One of the most widely cited statistical measures of economic inequality is the GINI coefficient (also referred to as Gini Index or Gini ratio). It measures the dispersion of income distribution or distribution of wealth among the members of a population with a value ranging from zero (0) denoting perfect equality and one (1) denoting maximal inequality (or 0% to 100%). The closer the value of the coefficient is to 1, the higher is the inequality of income distribution, and the closer the value of the GINI coefficient is to 0; the more equal is the distribution of income. Countries with highly unequal income distribution usually have a GINI coefficient between 0.50 and 0.70, and those with relatively equal distributions have a GINI coefficient between 0.20 and 0.35, according to some economists and analysts.

It is important to point out that the GINI coefficient is used to measure income inequality at the national level. At the global level, per capita gross domestic product (GDP) is used for comparing differences in income between countries.

1.2 State of Global Economic Inequality

Global economic inequality is one of the greatest challenges in the world today. *What are its causes and consequences? What has been done to narrow the economic gaps between countries?* Before addressing these questions, let us first establish how countries are classified.

The World Bank classifies countries by income levels and categorizes them into four income groups – low income, lower-middle income, upper-middle income, and high income. The classification of a country is determined by that country's gross national income (GNI) per capita in the current US dollar (US$) that the World Bank adjusts annually to account for inflation. As a result, a country's classification may change (upward or downward).

Table 1 shows the 2020-2021 World Bank country classifications. It is important, however, to note that the World Bank has indicated that it has used the 2019 GNI numbers for the 2020-2021 income classifications and that these numbers do not reflect the impact of COVID-19 (corona virus disease 2019).

Table 1: Country Classifications (2020 - 2021)

Group	Income Level (GNI/Capita/$)
Low Income	Less than 1,036
Lower-Middle Income	1,036 – 4,045
Upper-Middle Income	4,046 – 12,535
High Income	Greater Than 12,535

[Source: The World Bank]

As per the World Bank's current classifications, 29 countries/territories are categorized as low income, 50 as lower-middle-income, 56 as upper-middle-income, and 83 as high incomes.

According to World Inequality Report 2018 (WIR 2018), income inequality has increased in nearly all regions of the world in recent decades, but it varies greatly among regions. The Report indicates that since 1980 income inequality has increased rapidly in North America, China, India, and Russia, but it has grown moderately in Europe. In 2016, the share of total national income accounted for just that nation's top 10% earners (top 10% income share) was 37% in Europe, 41%

in China, 46% in Russia, 47% in US-Canada, around 55% in Sub-Saharan Africa, Brazil, and India, and the top 10% in the Middle East capture 61% of national income (WIR 2018). Based on this high-income share (61%) captured by the top 10%, the Middle East is therefore viewed as the most unequal region in the world.

The aforementioned report reveals a surprising fact regarding the varying pace at which inequality levels have diverged among countries/regions. WIR (2018) states that the divergence in inequality levels has been particularly extreme between Western Europe and the United States, which had similar levels of inequality in 1980 but today are in radically different situations. While the top 10% income share was close to 10% in both regions in 1980, reports WIR 2018, it rose only slightly to 12% in 2016 in Western Europe while it shot up to 20% in the United States.

Like income inequality, wealth inequality has also risen. Citing an Oxfam report published in January 2016 as world leaders gathered in Davos, Switzerland, for the 46th World Economic Forum (WEF) from 20-23 January 2016, WEF (2016) states that the richest 1% hold over 50% of the world's wealth, and 62 billionaires own the same amount of wealth as 3.5 billion people, who make up the poorest half of the world's population. The WEF

(2016) has further quantified the amount by indicating that the wealth held by the 62 richest people on the planet is estimated at $1.76 trillion, a 44% increase from five years ago. Ironically, the 3.5 billion poorest people have seen their wealth shrink by over a trillion dollars, or 41%, in the same period (WEF, 2016). The chart below reproduces the direction of the share of global wealth for 2010-2015 for visualization purposes.

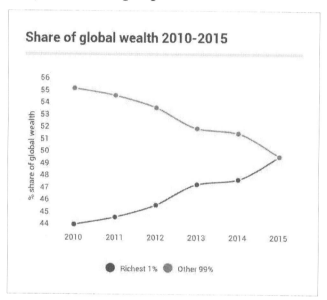

Figure 1: Share of Global Wealth 2010-2015
(Source: World Economic Forum)

The chart clearly shows the percentage increase in the wealth share for the richest 1% (bottom line) while the percentage wealth share for the other 99% (upper line) declines.

Commenting on the rise of wealth inequality, WIR (2018) posits that wealth inequality has risen at different speeds in different countries or regions. While the rise in wealth inequality has been very large in the United States, where the top 1% wealth share rose from 22% to 39% in 2014, the increase in top-wealth shares in France and the United Kingdom was more moderate over the past forty years (WIR 2018).

Wealth inequality has worsened in the United States in the most recent years. Inequality.org (2020) asserts that for the first time in U.S. history, the top twelve (12) U.S. billionaires surpassed a combined wealth of $1 trillion ($1.015 trillion to be exact) as of 13 August 2020. Commenting on this situation, Inequality.org (2020) states, "This is a disturbing milestone in the U.S. history of concentrated wealth and power. This is simply too much economic and political power in the hands of twelve people". Inequality.org further argues that from the point of view of a democratic self-governing society, this represents "an oligarchic Twelve or a Despotic Dozen." Facing this reality, many U.S. nationals ask, "Are we becoming a society of 'haves' and 'have nots'?"

It is also reported that top-wealth shares in China and Russia have risen in those countries, following their transitions from a communist system (planned economic system) to a more capitalist economic system. According to WIR 2018, the top 1% wealth share doubled in both China and Russia between 1995 and 2015, from 15% to 30% and from 22% to 43%, respectively.

This high level of concentration of wealth and power in the hands of a small group is very problematic because this minority can (and does) use their combined financial and political power to constrain governments' policies to reduce inequality and alleviate poverty.

Regarding wealth distribution among individuals within countries and across regions of the world, the 2020 Forbes billionaires list reveals that most of the world's wealth is concentrated in the United States. According to the list, *Forbes* counted 2,095 billionaires in the world as of 18 March 2020. For illustration and comparison, Table 2 provides a list of the top 20 billionaires, their net worth, and countries of origin.

Table 2: 2020 Top 20 Billionaires

No.	Rank Name	Net Worth (US$)	Country
1	Jeff Bezos	$113B	United States
2	Bill Gates	$98B	United States
3	Bernard Arnault & Family	$76B	France
4	Warren Buffet	$67.5B	United States
5	Larry Ellison	$59B	United States
6	Amancio Ortega	$55.1B	Spain
7	Mark Zuckerberg	$54.7B	United States
8	Jim Walton	$54.6B	United States
9	Alice Walton	$54.4B	United States
10	Rob Walton	$54.1B	United States
11	Steve Ballmer	$52.7B	United States
12	Carlos Slim Helu & Family	$50.9B	Mexico
13	Larry Page	$49.1B	United States
14	Sergey Brin	$48.9B	United States
15	Francoise B. Meyers & Family	$48B	France
16	Michael Bloomberg	$38.8B	United States
17	Jack Ma	$38.2B	China
18	Charles Koch	$38.2B	United States
19	Julia Koch & Family	$38.2B	United States
20	Ma Huateng	$38.1B	China

[Source: Forbes.com – Billionaires]

As the Table shows, 14 of the top 20 billionaires are U.S. nationals, which represents a share of 70 percent. Only three of the 20 billionaires are from Europe (2 from France and 1 from Spain), which represents a share of 15%; two are from Asia (both of them from China), which is a share of 10%; and one from Mexico.

Regarding economic inequality in India, *The Economist* magazine (dated December 5, 2020) points out that over the past year, as India's economy has shrunk by around a tenth and tens of millions of Indians have lost jobs or sunk into poverty, the fortunes of the country's two richest people have swollen. Gautam Adani, whose conglomerate sprawls from ports to coal mines to food, has seen his personal wealth more than double, to some $32bn; Mukesh Ambani's riches, which derive from oil refining, telecoms, and retail, among other things, have grown by just 25%, albeit to an intimidating $75bn or so (*The Economist*). And the magazine sums up the situation like this: **The super-rich get richer, and everyone else gets poorer.**

The above data and assessment are clear evidence of unequal wealth distribution among people, countries, and regions.

With regards to all these billionaires, some people wonder whether they should *ethically* hold such a vast amount of wealth while thousands of people are either starving or dying of hunger or diseases. They also argue that these billionaires also use their economic and political power to prevent governments from implementing policies conducive to redistribution. In addition to paying little or no taxes, these billionaires obtain huge tax cuts. Oxfam International (2020) contends that getting the richest one percent to pay just 0.5 percent extra tax on their wealth over the next ten years would equal the investments needed to create 117 million jobs in sectors such as elderly and childcare, education, and health.

Oxfam International really puts economic inequality into perspective when it states, "The 22 richest men in the world have more wealth than *all* (emphasis) the women in Africa", and "The world's…billionaires have more wealth than the 4.6 billion people who make up 60 percent of the planet's population".

Although wealth inequality at the global level is a major concern, researchers acknowledge that it is impossible to provide a precise account because, as indicated by Piketty (2014), a substantial fraction of global financial assets is already hidden away in various tax heavens, thus limiting our ability to analyze the geographic distribution of global wealth. Even though the precise amount is unknown, reports Piketty, all the evidence indicates that the vast majority (at least three-quarters) of the financial assets in tax havens belong to residents of the rich countries.

How has the super-rich dealt with the criticism about their wealth?

The super-rich tends to ignore criticisms. They use their wealth to live a luxurious lifestyle and to ensure the financial security of the members of their families and other loved ones. Towards this end, they invest and reinvest a large portion of their wealth in different productive business activities.

In addition to doing what the above have done, some super-rich have made the decision to become philanthropists to appease their conscience. Aware of the high level of inequality and poverty around them and across the world, they make donations to support some charitable projects. For instance, The Richest reports that Gates established a $2 billion foundation with his wife Melinda that aims to increase the standard and quality of health care and education in different countries; Buffett has been donating $1.5 billion each year to the same foundation on the condition that the foundation gives away an equal amount to qualified beneficiaries, and he plans to give away most of his wealth before he passes away.

Chapter two will address one of the two questions posed earlier: *what are the causes and consequences of inequality?*

Chapter 2:
Causes and Consequences
of Inequality

The causes of economic inequality are numerous, but experts do not agree on all of them. However, they tend to agree on two, which according to them, increase income disparities within countries:

- **Returns to Private Investment**

Analysts indicate that when the rate of return to private investors and owners of capital is greater than the overall economic growth, it leads to economic inequality. This inequality, says Piketty (2014), expresses a fundamental contradiction, which he explains this way: "The entrepreneur [private investor and owner of capital] tends to become a rentier [a person living on unearned income], more and more dominant over those who own nothing but their labor. Once constituted, capital reproduces itself faster than output increases. The past devours the future".

Instead of saying "returns to private investment," some scholars use the phrase *Unequal ownership of capital.* And they argue that unequal ownership of capital has fueled economic inequality because it gives rise to *unequal returns* on capital which are, as stated by Piketty (2014), a force of divergence that significantly amplifies and aggravates the effects of inequality.

- **Declining Population Growth Rate**

The declining population growth rate among the overall population in the developed countries is considered as a major cause of inequality because "low economic growth combined with a declining population (in the developed world) contributes to higher concentrations of wealth and results in inequality."

It is important to note that the *global* population has increased even though population growth has declined in developed countries because the replacement rate is not negative in the developing world.

In addition to the two cases just described, several other factors have also contributed to economic inequality at the national and global levels. Among them are:

(i) *Privatizations.* Privatizations and increasing income inequality within countries are also mentioned as causes of the rise of wealth inequality among individuals. In this vein, WIR (2018) argues that increasing income inequality and the large transfers of public to private wealth occurring over the past forty years have yielded rising wealth inequality among individuals.

(ii) *Corruption.* Corruption is a major cause of inequality; it increases social inequities and exacerbates poverty. It is argued that corrupt governments tend to make it difficult for citizens to acquire resources and wealth. (For a thorough analysis of the issue of *corruption*, see Germain, 2020).

(iii) *Population densities.* It is also argued that countries or regions with high population densities tend to overuse their resources, which makes it difficult for them to compete with less densely areas.

(iv) *Economic growth* is an important factor in consideration of inequality, and income distribution matters for growth. If the income share of the top 20 percent (the rich) increases, then GDP growth actually declines over the medium term, suggesting that the benefits do not trickle down, but an increase in the income share of the bottom 20 percent (the poor) is associated with higher GDP (IMF 2015). This is a significant difference that explains the importance of income distributions among population groups.

In their assessment of the relationship between growth, inequality, and income distribution, Rose-Ackerman & Palifka (2016) assert that high growth rates can coexist with rising inequality, with those at the bottom of the income distribution receiving few benefits and the majority of the income growth accruing to the top of the distribution.

(v) *Technology*. Technological progress is viewed as a positive factor because it usually leads to an increase in productivity. But it has also contributed to an increase in inequality, particularly in the United States and the United Kingdom, because it has changed the organization of the economy. In this respect, Banerjee & Duflo (2019) argue that a lot of the most successful inventions that came out of the high-tech revolution were 'winner take all' products.

This "winner-take-all (or if not all, most) economy, in which a few firms capture a large part of the market," partly explains the concentration of wealth and power in the hands of a few high-tech giants like Amazon, Microsoft, Google, Apple, and Facebook. That explains why Jeff Bezos of Amazon and Bill Gates of Microsoft are the two richest men in the world (see Table 2).

Commenting on the impact of digitization on employment, Banerjee and Duflo contend that as tasks from car painting to spreadsheet manipulation are done by computers or robots, highly educated workers who are adaptable and can program and install the robots will become more and more valuable, but other workers who can be replaced will find themselves without jobs unless they accept *extremely low salaries* (emphasis). In this view, they add, artificial intelligence will be the final nail in the coffin of these ordinary workers. This situation will lead to more inequality.

(vi) *National Government Policies* do play an important role in shaping inequality. It is argued that policies that focus on the poor and the middle class (such as access to better education and health care) can mitigate inequality.

(vii) *Globalization.* Although *trade* liberalization has been an engine for growth in some countries - including several developing countries referred to as emerging market developing countries (EMDCs) - it has also been a driver of income inequality in many other countries. Regarding the impact of globalization on income inequality in developing countries, Goldberg (2007) of Yale University and Pavcnick (2007) of Dartmouth posit that while globalization was expected to help the less skilled, who are presumed to be a locally relatively abundant factor in developing countries, there is overwhelming evidence that these are generally not better off, at least not relative to workers with higher skill or education levels. This observation is also true pertaining to the wages of unskilled workers in advanced/developed economies.

Inequality.org. (2015) has argued that income inequality within countries has increased virtually *everywhere* (emphasis) as a result of globalization. *Financial* liberalization has also contributed to a greater concentration of wealth in the hands of owners of capital (the already rich).

In its assessment of the adverse impacts of globalization on *small farmers,* the Food and Agriculture Organization of the United Nations (FAO) states that experience in recent decades has shown that non-subsidized small farms need agricultural prices that are sufficiently high for them not only to survive but also to invest and develop, a situation that *free trade in agriculture* clearly cannot offer the vast majority of the world's small farmers. On the contrary, says FAO (2001), continued free trade with its downward trend in real agricultural prices and its price fluctuations will condemn further hundreds of millions of small farmers and agricultural workers to stagnation, impoverishment, migration, and hence to unemployment and low wages, especially in developing countries but also to some extent in developed countries.

To prevent a misinterpretation of its assessment, FAO (2001) adds that it is not a question of choosing between globalization and non-globalization but of choosing between *blinkered liberal globalization* that blocks and excludes the poor and a carefully considered, *organized, and regulated globalization* that is beneficial to all and should receive broad-based support.

(For additional information on globalization, see Appendix I & II).

- **Is inequality desirable or undesirable?**

As shown in our analysis, both income inequality and wealth inequality has been on the rise across the globe for several decades, and this widening gap between the rich and the less fortunate has been a major concern for economists, policymakers, politicians, and other concerned individuals. Despite this concern, however, there is no unanimous position on the desirability or undesirability of economic inequality. According to several observers and analysts, including economists, inequality has both advantages and disadvantages.

Advantages.

> Some of the arguments in favor of inequality are:

> (i) *Incentives.* Inequality is necessary for providing incentives in a free market economy. According to this view, "there would be economic stagnation and lack of enterprise without a degree of inequality."

> (ii) *Rewards.* By rewarding hard work, productivity will increase because entrepreneurs will be more willing to take risks and start new businesses, which will lead to higher national output.

(iii) *Trickle-down effect.* When an entrepreneur sets a new business, some people gain extra income, and this can "trickle down to other people" in the forms of jobs and incomes to other workers.

(iv) *Growth.* It is argued that inequality drives growth, and rising levels of economic inequality often correlate with economic growth. It is important, however, to note that the benefits of growth are usually concentrated among a select few; they do not ipso facto 'trickle-down' to the poor.

(v) *Fairness.* Some analysts argue that inequality increases fairness, and "a society with pronounced economic inequality is fairer than a society with a generally equal wealth distribution." They further contend that "people deserve to keep higher incomes if their skills merit it."

Disadvantages.

The following arguments have been put forward against inequality.

(i) *Inequality stifles growth.* Commenting on the growth argument previously put forward in favor of inequality, some economists contend that "a degree of inequality can act as a positive influence on growth in the *short term* (emphasis), but empirical evidence shows a negative correlation between *long-term* growth rates and sustained economic inequality." In their attempt to explain how inequality 'stifles growth,' they argue that a high level of economic inequality means a higher level of poverty, and poverty is associated with increased crime and poor public health, which places burdens on the economy. They also add, "A widening rich-poor gap tends to increase the rate of rent-seeking and predatory-market behaviors [such as predatory pricing and predatory dumping] that hinder economic growth."

(ii) *Inequality increases crime.* Some researchers argue that studies have established a positive relationship between income inequality and crime. They point out that unequal societies have higher crime rates, and "inequality is the single factor most closely and consistently related to crime."

(iii) *Inequality decreases health.* It is argued that access to quality health care and healthy food is sometimes limited or unavailable to the impoverished members of society, which makes them more vulnerable to certain types of disease and a higher mortality rate.

(iv) *Inequality decreases education.* It is argued that the society-wide average level of education decreases in an economically unequal society. According to empirical research, a "one-point increase in the GINI coefficient (a measure of income inequality) translates into a 10% decrease in high school graduation rates…"

(v) *Economic inequality increases political inequality.* Some analysts contend that political power tends to be skewed in favor of a small wealthy group when wealth distribution becomes concentrated in the hands of that small group. According to them, high-income groups are in a position to manipulate government in their favor through corrupt practices and legal processes while the poor or working-class are less able to participate in the political process "as economic means become increasingly scarce."

(vi) *Inherited wealth.* Some observers argue that inherited wealth gives some people an "unfair" advantage in life, and "inheritance helps fuel rise in absolute wealth inequality."

The above pros and cons illustrate the divergence of opinions among analysts, including economists, on the desirability and/or undesirability of inequality. Some economists are of the opinion that inequality is beneficial and desirable for stimulating economic growth and improving the standard of living for members of society. They contend that inequality is a necessary part of any society. On the other hand, other economists argue that wealth concentrations in the hands of a small group of individuals result in the exploitation of the less fortunate members of society, hinder economic growth, and create societal problems.

Chapter 3:
Proposed Solutions to Inequality

A s extreme economic inequality has been considered "corrosive" to societies, several economists, policymakers, politicians, and institutions have been looking for ways to reverse the trend. Towards this goal, they have made several proposals.

- *Stop Illicit Financial Flows.* Inequality.org (2015) reports that developing countries lost $6.6 trillion in illicit financial flows from 2003 through 2012, with illicit outflows increasing at an average rate of 9.4 percent. By stopping these illicit outflows, the money could be used to reduce inequality through investment in human capital, infrastructure, and economic growth.

- *Progressive Income Tax.* As inequality has been worsening in rich countries, some economists and policymakers have suggested an increase in the tax rate of the top one percent of income earners (up to 65%). It is argued that this increase is justified because, according to Inequality.org (2015), the top one percent is not only capturing larger shares of national income, but tax rates on the highest incomes have also dropped.

Arguing in favor of a progressive tax, Piketty (2014) asserts that the right solution is a progressive annual tax on capital because this will make it possible to avoid an endless inegalitarian spiral while preserving competition and incentives for new instances of primitive accumulation. He further adds that this would contain the unlimited growth of global inequality of wealth, which is currently increasing at a rate that cannot be sustained in the long run and that ought to worry even the most fervent champions of the self-regulated market.

As the question of more taxes on the rich has taken center stage in both political and economic discourses, Banerjee & Duflo (2019) state that it seems to us that high marginal income tax rates, applied only to very high incomes, are a perfectly sensible way to limit the explosion of top income inequality, and they would not be extortionary because very few people will end up paying them. Top managers will simply not get these kinds of income anymore, they add.

People have taken different positions on the question of taxing the rich, and there is an ongoing debate among scholars over the issue because it involves a trade-off between economic growth and income redistribution. The skeptics argue that the tax on the rich lowers the growth rate, which has a negative impact on both workers and capitalists. The proponents, on the other hand, argue that the gap in income is so big (meaning high inequality), income redistribution through such a tax offsets some loss in growth. In other words, the benefit outweighs the cost. They also argue that the increase in growth does not necessarily "trickle-down." They are, therefore, willing to sacrifice some growth in favor of redistribution.

- *A Global Wealth Tax.* In an attempt to combat extreme economic inequality, Piketty (2014) has recommended a global wealth tax.

According to his proposal, countries around the world would tax personal assets of all kinds at graduated rates. Although skeptics have questioned the practicability of such a proposal, proponents argue that it makes sense to globalize the rules and standards if capitalism is going to be globalized.

- *Enforce a Living Wage.* Some observers and analysts advocate for a living wage. They contend that governments and corporations should establish and enforce a national living wage because all workers should earn enough to support themselves and their families. Inequality.org argues that low and unlivable wages are the result of worker disempowerment and concentration of wealth at the top – hallmarks of unequal societies.

- *Workers' Right to Organize.* The right of workers to organize has always been a cornerstone of more equal societies and should be prioritized and protected wherever this basic right is violated (Inequality.org). This organization further indicates that the right of workers to organize and bargain collectively for better pay and conditions is a global human rights priority.

- *Stop Labor Misclassification.* It is argued that companies worldwide have been replacing what was once permanent and stable employment with temporary and "contingent labor." These "contingent" or "precarious" workers fill a labor need that is permanent while being denied the status of employment (Inequality.org). In the United States, contends Inequality.org, this trend is called "misclassification," in which employers misclassify workers as "independent contractors" when they are actually employees. Some analysts refer to this practice as "labor abuses."

- *Open and Democratic Trade Policy.* Negotiating international trade agreements behind closed doors with only bureaucrats and corporate lobbyists present has to end because these old-style trade agreements are fundamentally undemocratic and put corporate profits above workers, the environment, health, and the public interest, argues Inequality.org (2015). As a result, conclude some analysts, a new, open, and transparent trade policy is needed.

- *Goal 10: Reduced Inequalities.* In 2015, the United Nations adopted 17 new "Sustainable Development Goals" as part of the 2030 Agenda for Sustainable Development. Goal 10: Reduced Inequalities focuses on the issue of inequality, considered by the United Nations as a persistent cause for concern within and among countries. The Goal 10 targets, *inter alia,* are:

(a) Ensure equal opportunity and reduce inequalities of the outcome by eliminating discriminatory laws, policies, and practices and promoting appropriate legislation, policies, and action in this regard.

(b) Adopt policies, especially fiscal, wage, and social protection policies, and progressively achieve greater equality.

- *A New and Real World Economics.* Critics of 'mainstream economics' have advocated for "new and real-world economics" because they view today's economists as "stuffy academics who value arcane economic theory above humanitarian values." Frustrated by the control of 'mainstream economists' over the discipline, some economists have left the profession, and fewer students have entered the field. In this regard, *The Economist* magazine (August 8th -14th 2020) reports that a former Federal Reserve researcher, Claudia Sahm, has chosen to "no longer identify" as an economist. She argues, reports *The Economist,* that the profession fails to nurture the young or listen to *outsiders.* A survey by the American Economic Association (AEA) found that only 31% of economists under the age of 44 felt valued within the discipline; this must be-off putting to youngsters beginning the long journey into the profession, and that makes them wonder if there is room for their ideas in a discipline that can seem hidebound, hierarchical and homogeneous *(The Economist).*

Critics of the present state of the economics profession include several winners of the Nobel

Prize for Economics. Among them are the late Milton Friedman, who argued that "economics has become increasingly an arcane branch of mathematics rather than dealing with real economic problems"; the late Vassily Leontief also argued, "Year after year economic theorists continue to produce scores of mathematical models and to explore in great detail their formal properties; and the econometricians fit algebraic functions of all possible shapes to essentially the same sets of data" (Fullbrook, 2007).

In respect to mathematical models, Piketty (2014) states that it is not the purpose of social science research to produce mathematical certainties that can substitute for open, democratic debate in which all shades of opinion are represented.

Although the debate over the economics profession is very *apropos*, it is beyond the purview of this study.

Effectiveness of Proposed Solutions

In its assessment of the proposed solutions to inequality, the World Bank posits that six policy areas have proved to be effective in reducing inequality:

- Early childhood development

- Nutrition interventions.

- Universal health coverage.

- Universal access to quality education.

- Cash transfers to poor families.

- Rural infrastructure – especially roads and electricity.

- Progressive taxation.

What explains the effectiveness of these policies?

The World Bank asserts that these six policies have shown to be effective in reducing inequality because they offer very few trade-offs between equity and efficiency and have worked repeatedly in different settings around the world. Although these policies are by no means the only paths to reduce inequality, they are those for which researchers have the most compelling body of evidence, adds the World Bank.

Although research shows that a high level of economic inequality is manifested in high levels of poverty in some groups of individuals within countries around the world, there had been a debate on the relationship between inequality and poverty. Before we move to Part Two of this study – Global Poverty -, it is important to address this issue of relationship.

Is there a Link between Inequality and Poverty?

As inequality and poverty are two different concepts, some analysts argued that empirical evidence had not been clear about the relationship between the two. To put the issue to rest, researchers such as Abigail McKnight at the Centre for Analysis of Social Exclusion, London School of Economics (CASE at LSE), investigated the link between inequality and poverty. They found that the "levels of income inequality and relative income poverty are strongly correlated across countries [and] so are changes in inequality and changes in poverty" (CASE at LSE, 2018). They also added that this strong correlation between income inequality and income poverty is positive.

Weil (2016) has established the relationship more directly when he says: For any given average level of income if income is distributed more unequally, more people will live in poverty. To make his point more convincingly, he provides this evidence:

In the year 2005, the average income per capita in India ($2,557) was 21% higher than the average income per capita in Pakistan ($2,112). But the fraction of the population living on an income of less than $1.25 per day was 41.6% in India, compared with only 22.5% in Pakistan. The reason for the difference was the distribution of income. Pakistan has a more equal distribution of income than India.

Aware of the strong link between inequality and poverty, international institutions – such as the United Nations, World Bank, OECD, Oxfam, and World Economic Forum – recommend that policies be set "to simultaneously tackle poverty and inequality in rich as well as poor countries." They recommend the approach of tackling the "twin goals" of reducing inequality and poverty simultaneously because they become convinced that policy cannot "successfully target poverty reduction … without addressing income inequalities" (CASE at LSE).

The linkage between inequality and poverty being established, the study will now move to Part Two –

Global Poverty - but before doing so, it is important to point out that the current public health and economic crises generated by the coronavirus pandemic (COVID-19) have further widened the economic inequality gaps between the "haves" and the "have nots." While these dual crises have negatively impacted ordinary people - especially low-income workers - around the world, the fortunes of billionaires have expanded considerably. According to the Institute for Policy Studies analysis of Forbes data, the combined wealth of all U.S. billionaires increased by $821 billion (28 percent) between March 18, 2020, and September 10, 2020, from approximately $2.947 trillion to $3.768 trillion (Inequality.org).

(For information on a dilemma generated by the dual health and economic crises in terms of policies, read Appendix II).

CONCLUDING COMMENTS

To put the issue of inequality into proper perspective, it is important to note that economists, analysts, and other observers have become concerned about economic inequality not because they are in favor of equal distribution of wealth and income, but because of the increasing gaps between the rich and the less fortunate. By inequality, they mean "inequality of opportunities." Individuals, as well as countries, possess different resources, skills, levels of education and therefore will continue to have different incomes and wealth.

Economic inequality has existed for centuries, and economists and policymakers are not advocating for its elimination. As previously indicated, some of them believe that inequality is beneficial and desirable for stimulating economic growth and improving the standard of living for members of societies, while others argue that wealth concentrations in the hands of a small group of individuals result in the exploitation of the less fortunate members of society, hinder economic growth and create societal problems. They are instead very concerned about the detrimental socio-economic and political consequences of an ever-widening economic gap among groups of societies and countries. They are in favor of shrinking that gap for the well-being and good functioning of societies worldwide.

Part Two:
Global Poverty

Figure 2: Global Poverty Map

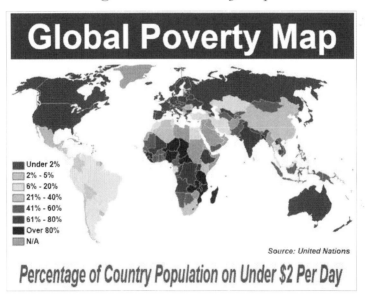

Chapter 4:
Poverty around the World

Global poverty is one of the very worst problems that the world faces today. The poorest in the world are often hungry, have much less access to education, regularly have no light, and suffer from much poorer health. To make progress against poverty is, therefore, one of the most urgent global goals (Roser & Ortiz-Ospina, 2019).

To address the problem of poverty and several other global issues, the United Nations adopted in 2015 a document titled "Transforming Our World: 2030 Agenda for Sustainable Development". The document is comprised of 17 Sustainable Global Development Goals (SDGs). "End poverty in all its forms everywhere" is the first of the 17 Goals.

Related to Goal 1 is Goal 2: "End hunger, achieve food security and improved nutrition and promote sustainable agriculture." The 2030 Agenda for Sustainable Development "promises to leave no one behind" with the priority of reaching the poorest members of the global society first. Like the United Nations, the World Bank Group "is committed to fighting poverty in all its forms."

Poverty exists in all countries, developing as well as developed, but its level of severity varies among countries, depending on the concept adopted. Before going into the analysis of the issue of global poverty per se, it is essential to understand what is meant by poverty and how it is measured.

4.1 Concepts of Poverty

Poverty is viewed differently by different entities, and people talk about some specific types of poverty, such as income or consumption poverty, shelter poverty, food poverty, asset poverty, and health poverty. In fact, there has been a debate on how to best define poverty. As there has not been an agreed-upon definition of the term, several working definitions have been adopted. The following two are provided for the purpose of this study:

- Poverty is an economic condition characterized by a lack of both money and basic necessities, such as food, water, utilities, and housing;

- Poverty is the inability of people to afford an adequate standard of living.

Although both definitions generate considerable controversial debates, the second one - which is broader and more generic - is more subject to interpretation because the meaning of *adequate standard of living* varies between countries and over time. Economic standards, based on income levels and access to basic human necessities, are generally used to define poverty, and absolute/extreme poverty and relative poverty are used as methods of measurement.

How do the concepts of extreme/absolute poverty and relative poverty differ?

Absolute or extreme poverty refers to the situation of being unable or only barely able to satisfy basic human needs - such as food, water, clothing, and shelter. As per this definition, absolute poverty focuses on the biological needs of people. The World Bank has specified a minimum amount of income needed to satisfy these basic needs. Using 2011 purchasing power parity (PPP), the

World Bank set the amount at $1.90 per day in 2015. This required *minimum* amount henceforth became the updated *international extreme poverty line,* which is an arbitrary international real income measure used as a basis for estimating the proportion of the world's population that lives at bare levels of subsistence. In calculating the international poverty line, the PPP is used to provide more accurate comparisons of living standards among countries.

Individual countries also set their own *national poverty line* deemed appropriate for their own countries. Some national poverty lines are calculated from the *minimum consumption* levels, while other national poverty lines are based on *relative consumption* levels.

With regard to the adopted concept of absolute/extreme poverty, some specialists argue that basic needs should not be limited to biological needs. They assert that a minimum standard of health care and education should also be included. In this vein, the United Nations (UN) states in its paper "Ending Poverty": "Poverty entails more than the lack of income and productive resources to ensure sustainable livelihoods. Its manifestations include hunger and malnutrition, limited access to education and other basic services, social discrimination and exclusion, as well as the lack of participation in decision-making".

Critics of the absolute poverty measurement argue against the pure monetary definition of poverty (set at $1.90) because "it fails to factor in the quality of life." The UN has created alternative measures such as the Human Development Index (HDI) that factors health and education.

Relative poverty is the inability of someone to afford what other people have; it is a comparison with the economic situation of other people around him or her. This level of poverty changes based on context and is a moveable guidepost that is difficult to measure because people usually want to "keep up with the Jones." According to Sachs (2005), relative poverty is generally construed as a household income level below a given proportion of average national income; the relatively poor, in high-income countries, lack access to cultural goods, entertainment, recreation, and to quality health care, education, and other perquisites for upward social mobility.

At the European Union (EU) level, the notions of absolute and relative poverty are both used to describe poverty; and since 2010, the composite notion of Risk of Poverty or Social Exclusion, which brings together relative monetary poverty, material deprivation, and exclusion from the labor market, is also used (https://www.eapn.eu/what-is-poverty/poverty-what-is-it/).

Although the difference between the concepts of absolute (extreme) poverty and relative poverty does not matter to people experiencing poverty in their daily lives, it is very significant to economists and other scholars in their analysis of economic inequality and poverty. That said, this study focuses on poverty in the sense of *extreme poverty* because that is what institutions such as the United Nations and the World Bank mean when they say that they want to "end" or "eradicate" poverty. This concept is adopted because it is measurable.

How is poverty measured?

Different methodologies are used to measure poverty. For instance, the World Bank uses income and consumption. "OurWorldInData" goes beyond standard economic indicators to consider aspects such as education, health, and human rights. To aggregate various aspects of well-being into a single metric, the Oxford Poverty & Human Development Initiative (OPHI) published the Multidimensional Poverty Index (MPI), which is "widely used around the world and currently covers over 100 low and middle-income countries" (Roser

& Ortiz-Ospina, 2019). In the European Union (EU), people falling below 60% of median income are said to be "at-risk-of monetary poverty" (https://www.eapn.eu/what-is-poverty/how-is-poverty-measured/).

For consistency and practicality, and to be able to evaluate the success or the failure of governments and the international community to "eradicate extreme poverty" around the world, this study uses the World Bank's measurement that sets the *international extreme poverty line* at $1.90 and below per day. This measurable approach provides a way to compare living standards within countries more accurately.

4.2. State of Poverty around the World

While global poverty rates have been cut by more than half since 2000, one in ten people in developing regions still lives on less than US$1.90 a day – the internationally agreed poverty line, and millions of others live on slightly more than this daily amount. Significant progress has been made in many countries within Eastern and Southern Asia, but up to 42 percent of the population in Sub-Saharan Africa continues to live below the poverty line, states the United Nations (https://www.un.org/en/sections/issues-depth/poverty/).

The UN further indicates that 55% of the world's population have no access to social protection, more than 736 million people lived below the international poverty line in 2015, and around 10 percent of the world population is living in extreme poverty and struggling to fulfill the most basic needs like health, education, and access to water and sanitation.

Although the World Bank has set the international poverty line at $1.90 per day, it also uses other measurements of poverty to reflect some groups of countries' national poverty lines. For the lower-middle-income countries, it uses $3.20 and $5.50 for the upper-middle-income countries. It also "measures poverty across a multidimensional spectrum that includes access to education and basic infrastructure." In this regard, the World Bank (https://www.worldbank.org/en/topic/poverty/overview) states that at higher poverty lines, 24.1 percent of the world lived on less than $3.20 a day and 43.6 percent on less than $5.50 a day in 2017. The World Bank also indicates that in 2018 half of the poor are children; about 70 percent of the global poor aged 15 and over have no schooling or only some basic education. It further adds that women represent a majority of the poor in most regions and among some age groups.

Taking the economic effects of the current global health crisis into consideration, the World Bank asserts in the same document that extreme global poverty is expected to rise in 2020 for the first time in over 20 years as the disruption of the COVID-19 pandemic compounds the forces of conflict and climate change. It further indicates that many people who had barely escaped extreme poverty could be forced back into it by the convergence of COVID-19, conflict, and climate change; and a preliminary estimate, incorporating the effects of the COVID-19 pandemic, projects that an additional 88 million to 115 million people will be pushed into extreme poverty, bringing the total between 703 and 729 million.

Reflecting on the state of global poverty and the countries at the bottom, Collier (2007) argues that the global poverty picture is confused and conceals a divergent pattern. He posits that for some countries to do relatively better, others must do relatively worse, but the decline of the countries now at the bottom is not just relative. It is often absolute, and many of these countries are not just falling behind; they are falling apart.

According to Roser & Ortiz-Ospina (2013, revised in 2017 & 2019), most people in the world live in poverty, two-thirds of the world's population lives on less than $10 per day, and every tenth person lives on less than $1,90 per day.

Although this study uses the $1.90 a-day measurement of international poverty, it is important to note that some analysts argue that the International Poverty Line is "extremely low." For instance, Roser & Ortiz-Ospina assert that living conditions well above the International Poverty Line can still be characterized by poverty and hardship. In this vein, the European Anti-Poverty Network (EAPN), commenting on the state of poverty in the **European Union** (EU), affirms that poverty in the EU is a real problem that brings misery to the lives of many people, curtails their fundamental rights, limits the opportunities they have to achieve their full potential, brings high costs to society, and hampers sustainable economic growth.

Furthermore, EAPN, citing Eurostat of January 2018, reports that in spite of the overall wealth of the European Union, poverty in the EU is still at a relatively high level and rapidly increasing, with 17.3% of the EU-28 population, that is almost 87 million people, at risk of relative income poverty, more than 118 million people or 23.5% of the EU-

28 population at risk of poverty and social exclusion, 7.5% is severely materially deprived, and 10.5% is living in households with very low work intensity.

In the **EU**, as previously indicated, people falling below 60% of median income are said to be "at-risk-of monetary poverty." "People are considered to be "At Risk of Poverty or Exclusion" if they are at risk of relative monetary (AROP indicator) and/or severely materially deprived (SMD indicator) and/or living in households with very low work intensity" (EAPN).

Commenting on the depth or severity of poverty in the EU, EAPN states that it is not the same in all Member States. Although the depth of poverty for the EU as a whole in 2016 was 25%, it ranges from as low as 13.9% in Finland to as high as 31.9% in Greece and 36.2% in Romania; in Italy, this rate jumped from 23.2% in 2008 to 31.6% in 2016, while in Slovakia it jumped from 18.1% in 2008 to 26.1% in 2016 (EAPN, using data from Eurostat).

In the **United States,** the U.S. Census Bureau uses two measures to count people in poverty – the official poverty measure and the supplemental poverty measure - which are based on estimates of income needed to cover "basic needs." It uses a set of income thresholds (dollar amounts) to determine "poverty thresholds," meaning national/federal poverty lines. The thresholds vary according to the size of a family and the ages of its members, and these thresholds are updated every year to reflect inflation. If a family's total income before taxes falls below the family's threshold, every member of that family is considered in poverty, and when a family's total cash income falls below 50% of its poverty threshold, the members of that family are considered in "deep poverty." The concept of *deep poverty* in the United States may be understood as being comparable to the concept of *extreme international poverty*.

PovertyUSA.org (https://povertyusa.org/facts#:~:text=Poverty-thresholds) reports that the poverty threshold (national poverty line) in 2018 for an individual was $12,784; for two people, the weighted average threshold was $16,247; for three people, it was $19,985; for four people, it was $25,985. It also indicates that 38.1 million people lived in poverty, which means that those making less than the Federal government's official poverty rate represented 11.85% of the population in 2018. What is worse, states PovertyUSA.org, 5.3% of the population – or 17.3 million people – live in *deep* poverty, with incomes below 50% of their poverty thresholds, and 29.9% of the population – or 93.6

million people – live close to poverty, with incomes less than two times that of their poverty thresholds.

It might be very difficult for many individuals to imagine that people are living on less than $2.00 a day, but more than 736 million people around the world actually live in this state of poverty. The **United Nations** (https://www.un.org/en/sections/issues-depth/poverty/) provides an assessment of people living in extreme poverty ($1.90 or less per day) across the globe as follows:

- 736 million people lived below the international poverty line of US$1.90 a day in 2015.

- In 2018, almost 8 percent of the world's workers and their families lived on less than US$1.90 per person per day.

- Most people living below the poverty line belong to two regions: Southern Asia and Sub-Saharan Africa.

- High poverty rates are often found in small, fragile, and conflict-affected countries.

- As of 2018, 55 percent of the world's population have no access to at least one social protection cash benefit.

The above account of global poverty is very somber, but the United Nations has also acknowledged that some significant progress has been made in reducing poverty over the past decades, especially in many countries within Eastern and Southeastern Asia. More specially, it states that "in 2015, 10 percent of the world's population lived at or below $1.90 a day [which is] down from 16 percent in 2010 and 36 percent in 1990…However, the decline has slowed".

World Bank (2020, January 7th) has expressed a similar view regarding the slowing pace of the decline by stating that from 1990 to until 2015, extreme global poverty declined, on average, by a percentage point, but from 2013 to 2015, poverty declined only by 0.6 percentage points per year, and initial estimates for 2018 show that extreme poverty dropped just 1.4 percentage points in the three years between 2015 and 2018.

The state of global poverty would not be complete without taking into consideration the shocks of the coronavirus pandemic, which has adversely impacted global productions, global value supply chains, global financial markets, and global workforce (inter alia) because of market disruptions, firm shutdown measures, and lockdowns. Taking into account the impact of coronavirus disease 2019 (COVID-19), World Bank (2020, April 16th) forecasts that for the first time since 1998, poverty rates will go up as the global economy falls into recession and that the ongoing COVID-19 crisis will erase almost all the progress made in the last five years. Per capita incomes are expected to decline by 3.6%, which will tip millions of people into extreme poverty this year (World Bank, 2020 – June 8).

Having explained the different concepts of poverty, examined the state of poverty around the world, the next chapter will address the causes and consequences of poverty.

Chapter 5:
Causes and Consequences
of Poverty

As poverty is mainly the result of how society is organized and how resources are allocated among people, societal organization and allocation of resources are therefore the two principal causes of poverty. To be more precise, some of the cited cases and consequences are:

- *Inequality* is a major cause because it tends to marginalize groups of people and leave them with little or no resources and without any voice in society.

- *Conflict* also leads to poverty because large-scale and protracted conflicts/wars "can grind society to a halt, destroying infrastructure and cause people to flee [with only] the clothes on their backs," which forces them to become refugees at the mercy of others.

- *Poor healthcare system.* Extreme poverty and poor health often go hand in hand; in countries where health systems are weak, easily preventable, and treatable, illnesses like malaria, diarrhea, and respiratory infections can be fatal, and when people must travel far distances to clinics or pay for medicine, it drains already vulnerable households of money and assets and can tip a family from poverty to extreme poverty (Concern Worldwide USA, 2020).

- *Climate change.* Though some individuals have denied the existence and negative effects of climate change, the World Bank (https://www.worldbank.org/en/topic/poverty/overview) reports that climate change, according to new research estimates, will drive 68 million to 132 million people into poverty by 2030. One of the reasons cited is that many of the destitute depend on agriculture for their livelihoods, and when climate change or disasters (such as droughts, earthquakes, and floods) leave them without food, they fall further into poverty. It is estimated that about 132 million of the global poor live in areas with high flood risk.

The General Assembly of the United Nations, in its document A/C.2/73/L.9 of 18 October 2018, reaffirms that climate change is one of the greatest challenges of our time, that its adverse impacts undermine the ability of all countries to achieve sustainable development, that increases in global temperature, sea-level rise, ocean acidification, and other climate change impacts are seriously affecting coastal areas and low-lying coastal countries…and that the survival of many societies and the biological support systems of the planet is at risk, which further threatens food security and efforts to eradicate poverty.

- *Low levels of education.* Education is often considered a "great equalizer" because it can open doors to many opportunities, including jobs, resources, and skills needed to prosper in life. However, low levels of education and skills prevent people from accessing those opportunities and participating fully in societal activities.

- *Poor infrastructure and isolation.* A lack of infrastructure (such as roads, bridges, and ports) leads to the isolation of some regions, especially the rural areas, from major cities and economic zones. This isolation makes it difficult (if not impossible) for people living in those areas to have access to essential services (such as education, health, and transportation) and to escape poverty.

- *Lack of Government Support.* Contrary to most developed countries where governments provide some safety net to their nationals in need in the form of social welfare programs, most governments in developing countries do not do so for several reasons, usually the lack of resources and unwillingness to provide such services. It is argued that sometimes international donors prevent them from implementing social programs or force them to curtail those programs for the sake of "austerity" or as a "condition for receiving further financial assistance." This deprivation of a social safety net (for whatever reason) engenders more poverty, especially extreme poverty.

- *Size of family.* It is argued that large families tend to be at greater risk of poverty because they have higher costs of living and lower average incomes.

- *Social Exclusion.* Exclusion consists of dynamic, multi-dimensional processes driven by unequal power relationships interacting across four main dimensions – economic, political, social, and cultural – and at different levels, including individual, household, group, community, country, and global levels (World Health Organisation).

  Social exclusion is a major cause of poverty because it limits people's access to resources and opportunities and impedes their participation in normal economic, social and cultural activities, which leaves them marginalized. In other words, social exclusion prevents the attainment of "common good," defined as "the sum total of social conditions which allow people, either as groups or individuals, to reach their fulfillment more fully and more easily." (Common good has a completely different meaning in economics, but this definition is contextually more appropriate).

In a paper titled "Economic Development vs. Social Exclusion," Jeannette Sutherland (World Bank 2001) states, "Income disparities are found among racial groups in each of Brazil's five regions. Data show the North and Northeast, where Afro-Brazilians predominate, have the highest inequality rates along with the lowest income and economic activity levels in the country". The paper also points out that infant mortality rates and life expectancy at birth in the Northeastern states (predominantly black) are still worse today than the figures attained by the Southern states (predominantly white) in 1950. These citations clearly illustrate the negative impacts of social exclusion and racial discrimination on inequality and poverty.

The paper concludes, "Brazil –and the entire Latin American region – must decisively seek to eliminate the vast disparities that exist among its citizens. The practice of social exclusion, clearly linked to poverty and to poverty-stricken groups, will soon become more of a liability than an asset to the elite".

- *Corruption* – the misuse/abuse of entrusted power for private gain – creates and maintains poverty, particularly in developing countries.

It impedes governments' ability to implement policies conducive to development and poverty alleviation; it increases inequities, hinders economic growth and development (which would improve the poor's living standards); it diverts resources needed to provide essential services and exacerbates poverty. (See Germain 2020).

- *Political instability* is a major cause of poverty because periodic social upheavals, arms struggles, and coups d'état discourage domestic and foreign investment and the implementation of policies that might be conducive to growth and development.

- *Consumerism/Overconsumption.*

Consumerism - an ever-expanding consumption of goods – stands for consumer-driven societies by placing consumption at the center of economic growth and development. While consumption is necessary and might serve as an engine of economic growth (depending on the relationship between consumption and production), consumerism often leads to overconsumption, which might become a predicament for millions of people around the world.

It is, for instance, argued that overconsumption by the "haves" leads to waste of resources and deprives the "have nots" of their fair share of available resources. Consumerism/overconsumption, in this case, is viewed as a major cause of poverty. In addition to being considered as a waste of resources by many observers and analysts, overconsumption of food – for example – creates a "wasteful" industry: the *weight-loss* industry. It is hard for the poor, deprived of food, basic healthcare, and dying of hunger, to comprehend why people have overconsumed in the first place and then paid billions of dollars to lose extra weight.

According to MarketsandMarkets (http://www.marketsandmarkets.com/Market-Reports/weight-loss-obesity-management-markets-1152.html), the Weight Loss and Weight Management Market is estimated to reach US$ 303.81 billion by 2027 from US$ 175.94 billion in 2017, at a CAGR (compounded annual growth rate) of 6.9%; the growth of this market is in the majority attributed to the growing rate of obesity, increasing prevalence of lifestyle diseases, and increasing number of bariatric surgeries. The costs to treat these "lifestyle diseases" due to overconsumption are viewed as a form of overuse of resources and deprivation of resources to the poor. (Obesity might have some medical causes).

Food waste in a broader sense, the U.S. Department of Agriculture (USDA) asserts that food waste in the United States is estimated at between 30-40 percent of the food supply, an estimate corresponding to approximately 133 billion *pounds* and $161 billion worth of food in 2010. (These numbers are based on USDA's Economic Research Service of 31 percent food loss at the retail and consumer levels). USDA also adds that this amount of waste has far-reaching impacts on society: 1) Wholesome food that could have helped feed families in need is sent to landfills; 2) land, water, labor, energy, and other inputs are used in producing, processing, transporting, preparing, storing, and disposing of discarded food. At the global level, 1.3 billion *tons* of food is lost or wasted every year, according to The World Counts (https://www.theworldcounts.com/challenges/con sumption/foods-and-beverages/food-waste-facts/story.

The United Nations Environment Programme (UNEP) states that roughly 30 percent of the food produced worldwide is lost or wasted every year; over 30 percent of adults globally are estimated to be overweight or obese, and 12.9 percent of the population in developing regions suffer from chronic hunger. A reduction (or better the elimination) of the afore-mentioned waste of resources would greatly improve the plight of the "have nots."

It is also argued that current overconsumption, especially in the rich/developed countries, will eventually outpace the sustainable capacity of the ecosystem and leads to environmental degradation and depletion of many global natural resources, such as energy, biomass, genetic diversity, raw materials, drinking water, and groundwater.

- Technocratic Illusion

The conventional approach to economic development, to making poor countries rich, is based on a *technocratic illusion*: *the belief that poverty is a purely technical problem* (emphasis) amenable to such technical solutions as fertilizers, antibiotics, or nutritional supplements (Easterly, 2013). This same belief, states Easterly, is prevalent amongst others who combat global poverty, such as the Gates Foundation, the United Nations, and the United States and United Kingdom aid agencies.

Easterly (a former senior research economist at the World Bank) argues that the technocratic approach ignores the real cause of poverty which is *the unchecked power of the state against poor people without rights* (emphasis). He further argues that by this technocratic illusion, the technical experts unintentionally confer new powers and legitimacy on the state as the entity that will implement the technical solutions.

Easterly argues that the word *technocracy* is a synonym for *authoritarian development,* which means "rules by experts." And he concludes his analysis as follows:

"The technocratic illusion is that poverty results from a shortage of expertise, whereas poverty is really about a shortage of rights. The emphasis on the problem of expertise makes the problem worse. The technical problems of the poor (and the absence of technical solutions for those problems) are a *symptom* of poverty, not a *cause* of poverty."

- *Blaming the poor (laziness).* Some individuals blame the poor for their economic misfortune. "People are poor because they are lazy. How do we 'know' they are lazy? Because they are lazy". Promoters of these interpretations, according to Sachs (2005), rarely understand that low productivity results not from laziness and lack of efforts but from lack of capital inputs to production. African farmers are not lazy, but they do lack soil nutrients, tractors, feeder roads, irrigated plots, storage facilities, and the like (Sachs, 2005).

Is the laziness argument based on fact or prejudice?

Sachs (2005) provides this unequivocal answer: Stereotypes that Africans work little and therefore are poor are put to rest immediately by spending a day in a village, where backbreaking labor by men and women is the norm. To corroborate his answer, he uses a survey by World Values Survey in which households around the world were asked the same questions in order to permit comparisons of cultures and values. "When asked in 2000…whether it is especially important for children to be encouraged at home to learn 'hard work,' 61 percent of Americans said yes, whereas 80 percent of Nigerians, 75 percent of South Africans, and 83 percent of Tanzanians responded affirmatively". This is a piece of clear and measurable evidence that the laziness argument is based on prejudice rather than fact.

In addition to the above, civil war, historical colonialism, bad governance, religious affiliations, political systems, racism, ethnicity, and "dependence on the extraction and export of natural resources" are also mentioned as factors that have contributed to poverty.

This chapter has identified and analyzed some of the major causes and consequences of poverty. The next chapter will examine the question: *what to do to resolve or at least alleviate the problem?*

Chapter 6:
Combating Global
Poverty

Recognizing the global nature of poverty and its impacts on the less privileged, the United Nations, the World Bank, and several other institutions are committed to working towards a reduction in the level of poverty around the world. In this regard, the United Nations (in its document A/C.2/73/L.9 of 18 October 2018) reaffirms that eradicating poverty in all its forms and dimensions, including extreme poverty, is the greatest challenge facing the world today, and it is committed to ensuring that no country or person is left behind.

Many development professionals and analysts have criticized the notion of "no country or person is left behind" because it reflects a "paternalistic view of the marginalized" and a "paternalistic approach to development." Some have even wondered whether the notion is a strategy to control the destiny of lower-income and less-influential countries. As the focus must be on actions and results, *if successful,* that would be a major achievement by the international community.

Towards the attainment of the desired goal, the United Nations, in the above-cited document, *calls* upon the international community, including the Member States and the organization's development system, including the funds and programs and the *specialized* agencies to continue to accord the highest priority to poverty eradication. It also calls upon them to take measures to urgently address the root causes and challenges of poverty in all its forms and dimensions, including extreme poverty, hunger, and malnutrition.

Although the United Nations stresses the importance of eradicating *extreme poverty* (meaning people living on $1.90 or less per day), its overall goal is to "eradicate poverty in all its forms and dimensions." This overall goal is more aspirational than realistic because *relative poverty* (an aspect of poverty) is, by definition, an elusive (moveable) target.

The **World Bank**'s (a *Specialized Agency* of the United Nations) first goal is to "end extreme poverty globally." This approach is more pragmatic than to "eradicate poverty in all its forms and dimensions." To reduce global inequality, the World

Bank envisages "promote shared prosperity in every country," which is its second goal.

What does the World Bank mean by "shared prosperity"?

It means that the Bank "will work to increase the incomes and welfare of the poorer segments of society wherever they are, be it the poorest of nations or thriving middle- or high-income countries."

The two goals - end extreme poverty and promote shared prosperity - are inextricably linked. In this regard, the World Bank (https://www.worldbank.org/en/topic/isp/overview) states, "Without a significant reduction in inequality, especially in countries with high poverty and inequality, the world will not meet its goal to end extreme poverty by 2030". Will the World Bank meet this goal by 2030?

Before proceeding to specific proposed solutions to global poverty, it is important to comment on the goals of "eradicating (ending) global poverty in all its forms and dimensions" and "eradicating/ending extreme global poverty." The second one is *feasible* (though complicated) because it is specific and focuses on the elimination of extreme poverty (defined as living on $1.90 or less a day), but the first goal, as previously stated, is more aspirational because it encompasses two concepts (*extreme* poverty and *relative* poverty), and the latter is a moveable target.

In light of the above comment, this study will use the concept of *poverty reduction* instead of poverty eradication. It will also adopt the concept of *extreme poverty eradication* instead of poverty eradication in all its forms and dimensions. That said, let us now examine ways to reduce global poverty or eradicate/end extreme poverty.

6.1. Proposals to Combat Global Poverty

First, we have to acknowledge that finding solutions to global poverty is a complex and difficult task because there is no world government and no global consensus on how to deal with poverty. Although the international community promises to *leave no country behind* and is committed to helping countries reduce their level of poverty and eradicate extreme poverty, combating poverty essentially depends on governments' willingness and capability to implement policies conducive to that end. As we are living in a globalized world and most countries, especially the poorest, are not able to resolve the problem without international aid, several potential solutions have been put forward. Among them are:

- *Modernization of Agriculture*

As agriculture is the main economic sector in most developing countries and people depend on it for their livelihoods, teaching sustainable techniques to farmers and how to use more modern agricultural tools (equipment) has been proposed as a way to reduce poverty. The justification for this proposal is "when a country's natural resources are at their top potential, so is its economy." In this regard, World Poverty (https://world-poverty.org/solutionstopoverty.htm) asserts that improving the scientific training and equipment of farmers related to agriculture and natural resource management will help increase crop yields, conserve the environment, and improve the quality of life for farmers themselves and their families.

Other than instructing/training farmers, the Food and Agriculture Organization of the United Nations (FAO) has emphasized *agricultural commodity prices.* FAO (2001) posits that one powerful mechanism to reduce the huge occurrence of rural and urban poverty, under-consumption, and undernutrition that is slowing the development of the world economy lies in a *gradual, significant, and prolonged rise in agricultural commodity prices in developing countries.* This rise in prices, argues FAO, would serve to increase the earnings of under-equipped small farming communities and give them the means to survive, invest and develop, eliminate the source of extreme rural poverty and undernutrition, and curb agricultural migration and curb unemployment and poverty.

Modernization of agriculture could indeed be a solution, but how to finance it?

FAO (2001) provides an answer when it states that a gradual, significant, and prolonged rise in agricultural commodity prices in developing countries would raise the general level of wages, increase tax revenues and foreign currency earnings in the poorest developing countries, [thus] providing the means to invest in modernization and industrialization.

Mindful of the impacts of an increase in prices, FAO suggests that such a hike in prices should not be sudden, as its positive impact on food production, poor farmer income, and wages and other forms of earnings will not be very rapid, while the negative consequences of increased food prices for poor consumers and purchasers will be immediate; thus the rationale for its recommendation of a *gradual* increase in prices. Any increase in staple food commodity price should be sufficiently *gradual* for the positive impact on producers to always outweigh the negative impact on purchasers, says FAO.

- *Gender Equality*

Gender equality is viewed as a practical way to reduce poverty. It is argued that when women are allowed to participate in the economy, the country thrives. For that to occur, however, new laws must be adopted, social acceptance of women and proper childcare for their families are required, contend experts in gender equality.

It is also argued that educating girls and women can reduce poverty in developing as well as developed countries because a woman's degree of education is linked to the age at which she marries and has children, to her economic opportunities, and to her social standing.

- *Access to Clean Water*

Having access to clean water that is not only safe to drink but also close to people's homes is considered an important factor in improving people's quality of life because in many developing countries, people, especially women and girls, spent hours fetching water. To emphasize the importance of this factor, some observers posit that "investing in clean wells and water systems can not only ensure the safety of a country's citizens but can free up their time, allowing them to better participate in the economy."

- *Good Healthcare*

It is argued that good healthcare is essential to alleviating poverty because when people are healthy, they can better contribute to their country's economy and participate in socio-cultural activities in their communities.

- *Education*

Education is viewed as an effective tool in combatting poverty. Therefore, it has been proposed to make it a priority in order to lift people and countries out of poverty. To be successful, argue the proponents, better school systems and better trained and paid teachers are required. Good nutrition for students must also be integrated into proposed reforms because it is difficult for malnourished or hungry children to absorb new knowledge. This dilemma is more acute in developing than developed countries.

- *International Aid*

Many analysts, policymakers, and development specialists have proposed international aid as a means to combat poverty despite its well-documented ineffectiveness. Their argument is that many countries are not able to lift themselves out of poverty without foreign aid. They assert that foreign aid will improve the global quality of life.

The above arguments put forward by the proponents of foreign aid are valid, but the economic situation of most recipient countries has not improved despite the enormous amount of aid. Several reasons explain this failure: 1) foreign aid comes with conditions ("conditionalities") that are often difficult (if not impossible) to meet; 2) some countries do not have the proper structure to absorb the aid, and most importantly, 3) the level of corruption in recipient countries is so high, the aid never reaches the intended target, meaning the poor; it has instead served as a major source of enrichment for corrupt actors.

Regarding the issue of "conditionalities," Germain (2020) points out a dichotomy when he states that national public officials usually (sometimes rightfully) complain about international aid "conditionalities" imposed on them by donors, but when the aid comes *without* preconditions or oversight corrupt actors tend to embezzle the funds, which raises a serious question of credibility and accountability.

To circumvent the problem of corruption, international donors - in many instances - have channeled the aid to non-governmental agencies (NGOs). Despite the large number of public funds donated to and channeled via the NGOs to circumvent corrupt national officials, the outcomes are not noticeably better (Germain, 2020). The outcomes have not improved because "waste, mismanagement, fraud, and corruption also plague charities, non-governmental organizations and aid agencies (*America-The Jesuit Review*, 2018). Furthermore, these agencies lack transparency and accountability.

Some researchers think that aid can actually make things worse: aid may be an inducement to rebellion and to coups because capturing the state becomes more valuable; in the societies of the bottom billion, aid is probably the key part of what is sometimes called the 'rents to sovereignty' – the payoff to power (Collier, 2007).

The above observations on the ineffectiveness of foreign aid in significantly reducing poverty in developing countries do not mean that international assistance is not needed or should be discontinued because the argument that "many countries are not able to lift themselves out of poverty without foreign aid" is accurate. But the aid should be used to accelerate the economic development process, which would mitigate aid dependency and alleviate poverty (Germain, 2020). Moreover, transparency, accountability, better performance, control of corruption, and improvement in the quality of foreign assistance are prerequisites for the effectiveness of international aid.

- *Global Trade*

Global trade has been proposed as one of the potential solutions to poverty because it "will help fuel the struggling nation's economy and create more jobs." It is argued that both developed as well as developing countries will benefit in the sense that "the wealthy country gains a new trading partner, and the developing gains a sustainable way to grow its economy."

The above-proposed solution sounds good in theory, but in practice, it does not always work this way because global trade is not necessarily a "win-win" activity; it often involves winners and losers. When influential and powerful nations believe that the rules are no longer beneficial to them, they use *rapport de force* (meaning the influence and efficacy of the entities involved) to challenge and change them. The current trade conflict between large countries, especially the ongoing tensions between the United

States and China, corroborates the controversial nature of global trade (See Appendix I).

In response to political pressure and interest groups, governments often adopt trade policies to restrict foreign trade and protect domestic markets. As economics and politics are intertwined, an enduring debate in economics is over the extent to which governments should intervene in the economy.

- *Brain Drain*

Developed countries have been imposing severe restrictions on the immigration of less-skilled workers but have been at the same time encouraging high-skill migration –*brain drain* - and many highly-educated professionals from foreign countries, particularly developing ones, have used this opportunity to emigrate either for higher salaries, better living conditions, and lifestyles, or professional advancement and recognition. Docquier & Rapoport (2011) posit that the number of highly educated immigrants living in the OECD member countries (developed countries) increased by 70 percent during the 1990s and doubled for those originating from developing countries, compared to a 30 percent increase for low-skill immigrants.

The departure of these highly educated professionals has been detrimental to developing countries, which have used their limited resources to increase their human capital stock. When these highly skilled professionals leave their home countries, they take their acquired skills to already developed countries, which is, in fact, a transfer of scarce resources from poorer to richer countries. This flight of human capital is very problematic because the most educated, competent, and skilled professionals leave their countries of origin underdeveloped to foster more growth and development in more advanced nations. According to Docquier & Rapoport, high-skill emigration rates exceed 80 percent in countries such as Guyana, Jamaica, and Haiti and are above 50 percent in many African countries.

Regarding the migration of healthcare professionals from Africa, Tamrat (219) – president of St. Mary's University in Addis Ababa, Ethiopia – asserts that Sub-Saharan Africa has the highest levels of health worker migration in the world, and Ethiopia is one of the countries with the highest emigration of physicians in Sub-Saharan Africa. According to Berhan cited in Tamrat (2019), Ethiopia trained 4629 physicians (including 1153 specialists) between 1987 and 2006, but the public sector managed to retain only 20 percent or 932 professionals in the same period.

Ethiopia's case is a clear example of the negative impact of brain drain in terms of human resources and costs. It is very expensive for a developing country to educate medical doctors. According to one conservative estimate, states Tamrat (2019), nearly US$30,000 is lost for every medical school graduate who emigrates. The irony is that "Ethiopia's physician-to-population ratio [is] 1:21,000 [which] is also regarded as one of the lowest in Sub-Saharan Africa" (Tamrat 2019).

As high-skill migration has become the dominant pattern of international migration, it constitutes a serious source of concern in developing countries for several reasons: (1) the home country has lost human capital; (2) it also lost its investment in the education of these professionals, and potential revenue; (3) brain drain deprives the education system of qualified instructors/trainers; (4) the increasing outflow of healthcare professionals has negatively impacted the home country's healthcare system and the health of the population; (5) high-skill migration has increased inequality and poverty across and within developing countries, even though it may have some limited beneficial effects in the form of *remittances* (transfers of money by migrants to individuals in their respective home country).

As some scholars have addressed the issue of *brain drain* in relation to *remittances,* let us briefly examine the issue. The eminent and thought-provoking development economist William Easterly (2013) argues that "the idea of a disastrous brain drain has lost some credibility as evidence has accumulated on how much of their foreign incomes brain drainers have remitted back to their home countries." To justify this position, Easterly contends that the wage paid to the brain drainer [the highly-educated migrant] reflects the value of their contribution to *world output.* He also argues that when drainers leave low-wage jobs for high-wage jobs, they increase their productivity.

Framing the issue of *brain drain* and *remittances* in the context of national development (national GDP) *versus* world development (global GDP) is not in the interest of the most disadvantaged countries. To say that drainers "benefit not only themselves but the world development as a whole [and that] only a nationalist obsession would ignore such gains in global development" begs the following questions:

- *How beneficial is the increase in global GDP to the extreme poor surviving at or below the international poverty line of $1.90 per day?*

- *Are the remittances sent back home by "brain drainers" used to replace the loss of scarce human capital in the countries of origin?*

- *What happens to the promise "No country or person is left behind"?*

- *How to reconcile the facts that "Ethiopia is one of the countries with the highest emigration of physicians in Sub-Saharan Africa" and at the same time is one of the countries with "the lowest physician-to-population ratio in Sub-Saharan Africa"?*

- *Is there a supra-government/entity that is responsible for improving the quality of life of the poor living in the countries left behind?*

- *Do the benefits of remittances outweigh the cost and loss of highly-educated/skilled labor in low-income and struggling countries?*

The case of Ethiopia is a noteworthy example to illustrate the issue of "world development vs. national development" and the dilemma of the least developed countries in general in terms of brain drain. Ethiopia is one of the poorest countries in the world, was designated by the United Nations in 1971 as one of the "least developed countries," and has not been able to exit the LDC classification since (see Part III of this study). Putting the notion of nationalism aside, *is world development more beneficial to Ethiopians than national development that would alleviate poverty in their own country?*

To give priority to "the world development as a whole" over the development of the struggling LDCs is problematic because it will not advance the twin goals of "ending extreme poverty … and enhancing shared prosperity in *every country* (emphasis), which are also central elements of Sustainable Development Goals 1 (end poverty on all its forms everywhere) and 10 (reduce inequality within and among countries)" (World Bank, 2016). Furthermore, most development economists usually put emphasis on *health, education, sanitation,* and the like because social sector spending is viewed as 'pro-poor public expenditure (PPE)' that would increase human welfare and alleviate poverty in developing countries, particularly in low-income ones. Thus the question: health and education for whom?

The author's comments on brain drain do not imply that highly-educated professionals should not seek opportunities elsewhere to improve their quality of life or standard of living. It is incumbent on national governments to boost their economies – which is easier said than done – in order to retain those professionals.

To improve economic performance where the bottom billion live, however, should not be viewed as a "nationalist obsession." While it is important to have a worldview, it is also very important to bear in mind that people live within the borders of *specific countries* and not in a nebulous "global village." Globalization does not mean the end of nation-states. Although some of us (including this author) like the idea of being a "global citizen," *world citizenry* is an ideal, not a reality. Because we are citizens of defined nation-states, people still ask: "what country are you from?" The way that the idea of national development vs. world development is presented appears to prioritize development in high-income countries at the detriment of low-income ones.

The fact that high-skill emigration rates exceed 80 percent in countries such as Guyana, Haiti, and Jamaica and are above 50 percent in many African countries (as previously indicated) is not a good recipe for development in those countries.

Effective policies should be implemented to create jobs and stimulate local employment. Every LDC should be encouraged to implement what Germain (2020) calls a **MeRONS** (Measurable Result-Oriented National Strategy) to foster growth and development at home. Of course, it must also encompass a more productive use of the *remittances*, which would contribute to development. In order to be actionable and measurable, the strategy must clearly define the ultimate objective and explain how to achieve it.

Regarding remittances to LDCs in this global pandemic era, UNCTAD (2020, November 12) affirms that COVID-related travel bans, movement restrictions, and protectionist employment policies have cut migrant remittances to LDCs significantly, a situation likely to endure for the foreseeable future. This assessment represents additional proof that LDCs cannot count on remittances as a reliable source of revenue to improve the dire socio-economic situation at home.

Concluding Comments

Previously in this chapter, the study raises the question of whether the World Bank will reach its goal of ending extreme global poverty by 2030. The World Bank (https://worldbank.org/en/new/press-release/2020/10/07covid-19-to-add-as-many-as-150-million-extreme-poor-by-2021.print) provides its own answer to the question by stating that the convergence of the COVID-19 pandemic with the pressures of conflict and climate change will put the goal of ending [extreme] poverty by 2030 beyond reach without swift and substantial policy action. The Bank also posits that the COVID-19 pandemic is estimated to push an additional 88 million to 115 million people into extreme poverty in 2020, with the total rising to as many as 150 million by 2021, depending on the severity of the economic contraction. Instead of ending extreme poverty, the World Bank predicts that the global poverty rate could be about 7% by 2030.

While the pandemic has pushed more people around the world into extreme poverty ($1.90 or less per day), it has at the same time been a bonanza for the super-rich. For instance, Jeff Bezos - Amazon's boss - saw his wealth increase from $111bn in March 2020 to $185bn in December 2020, and the combined wealth of the world's ten richest people grew by 57%, to $1.14trn (*The Economist*, December 19, 2020).

COVID-19, pressures of conflict and climate change aside, Collier (2007) provided a more realistic assessment of the approach to global poverty when he stated: "Our approach toward the bottom billion has been failing. Many of these societies are heading down, not up, and they are collectively diverging from the rest of the world. If we let this continue, our children are going to face an alarmingly divided world and all its consequences". This assessment is still valid today. It is not enough to say "no country or person is left behind," a notion that many development specialists consider as a "paternalistic view of development." Is there a socio-political will and interest to make the slogan "no one or country left behind" a reality?

We have briefly raised the issue of remittances in the context of "world development vs. national development," but it is a very complex one that many researchers and scholars have studied in more detail. Remittances do act as a lifeline for the poor, and an increase in income for individuals and families that receive them and do have some positive effects in some countries. For instance, Migration Policy Institute (MPI, 2013) asserts that the inflow of foreign exchange from migrants increases the home country's creditworthiness and may allow them to secure more favorable terms of debt service, as lenders perceive a lower risk of default. MPI also states that migrants' remittances to their country of origin represent a major vehicle for reducing the scale and severity of poverty in the developing world.

This study raises the issue of *brain drain* in the context of "world development vs. national development" to point out that world development should not have priority over national development because people live in specific countries. When it is said that "migrants' remittances to their country of origin represent a major vehicle for reducing the scale and severity of poverty in the developing world," it is important to keep in mind that the *developing world* includes emerging economy countries such as China and India, as well as Latin American, African and Asian countries. The characteristics of individual states must be taken into account because not all of them are at the same stage of development.

The United Nations have designated 47 countries - including Ethiopia – in the developing world as the *least developed countries* (see Part III). The LDCs are different from the other developing countries (ODCs) in terms of their stage of development, scale, and severity of poverty. Although these countries have received migrants' remittances, the money has not contributed to growth and development in the home country because the individual recipients mainly use it for consumption. To foster development in these countries, most development economists usually recommend that they build up or increase their human capital (a highly-educated/trained labor force). But how to reconcile this recommendation with the ever-increasing number of "brain drainers"?

Part Three:
Poverty Reduction in the Least Developed Countries

Figure 3: Least Developed Countries

[Source: United Nations Conference on Trade and Development]

Chapter 7:
Poverty in the Least
Developed Countries

T he first part of this study has examined the issue of global economic inequality, identified its main causes and consequences, and analyzed some of the proposals to reduce the gaps between the "haves" and "have nots." After establishing the link between inequality and poverty, *Part Two* explained the main concepts of poverty, considered the state of poverty across the globe, examined its causes and consequences, and analyzed the proposals made to reduce the level of poverty around the world. Against this backdrop, *Part Three* will examine the issue of *poverty reduction* in a specific group of countries called the *least developed countries* (LDCs).

The United Nations Conference on Trade and Development (UNCTAD, 2016) indicates that global poverty is concentrated among this specific group of countries, which are falling further behind the rest of the world in terms of economic development. As of 2019, 47 countries have been classified by the United Nations as **Least Developed Countries (LDCs)**, and 21 of them have been on the LDC list since the inception of the LDC category in 1971. Most of the people that Paul Collier refers to as "the bottom billion" (those "that are dropping further and further behind the majority of the world's people, often falling into an absolute decline in living standards") live in LDCs. And it has been very difficult for these countries to exit this group once on the list.

As the global community has promised to reduce inequality, promote "shared prosperity," and eliminates extreme poverty throughout the world, this part of the study envisages to

(1) Find out what has been done to help reduce the level of poverty in LDCs;

(2) Identify and examine the effectiveness or ineffectiveness of the strategies implemented; and

(3) Determine why it has been so difficult to graduate from the LDC category.

Before investigating the above issues, this paper will first provide a brief background on the least developed countries.

7.1. The Least Developed Countries

The Least Developed Countries are a sub-group of the *Developing Countries* and are the world's most disadvantaged countries. Most of them are characterized by limited economic growth and export diversification and a lack of competitive industries, and exploitable natural resources. They also confront severe structural impediments to development and are vulnerable to natural disasters, such as droughts, floods, and hurricanes. They have few passable roads, few hospitals, and schools. According to UNCTAD, LDCs account for 15 of the 20 most aid-dependent countries in the world, due primarily to lack of savings.

What are the criteria used to classify a country as LDC?

The United Nations Committee for Development Policy (CDP) uses three main criteria for determining the LDC status:

- *Per- capita income*, which is based on a three-year average estimate of the gross national income (GNI) per capita, with a threshold of $1,035 for possible cases of addition to the list, and a threshold of $1,242 for cases of graduation from LDC status (UNCTAD,2016).

- *Human assets*, involving a composite index (the Human Assets Index) based on indicators of (i) nutrition (percentage of undernourished population); (ii) health (child mortality ratio); (iii) school enrolment (gross secondary school enrolment ratio); and (iv) Literacy (adult literacy ratio), as per UNCTAD (2016).

- *Economic vulnerability*, involving a composite index (the Economic Vulnerability Index) based on indicators of (i) natural shocks (index of the instability of exports of agricultural production; share of victims of natural disasters); (ii) trade-related shocks (index of instability of exports and services); (iii) physical exposure to shocks (share of population living in low-lying areas); (iv) economic exposure to shocks (share of agriculture, forestry, and fisheries in GDP;

index of merchandise export concentration); (v) smallness (population in logarithm); and (vi) remoteness (index of remoteness), as per UNCTAD (2016).

To be included in the group of LDCs, the threshold for all three criteria must be met, and the government of that country must give its consent. Without this consent, a country cannot be added to the list even if it is qualified and meets all three criteria. In this regard, UNCTAD (2017) states that qualification for addition to the list will effectively lead to LDC status only if the Government of the relevant country accepts this status. Table 3 provides a list of the current LDCs (as of 2019) together with the inclusion year for each country.

Table 3: Least Developed Countries

Country	Year of Inclusion
Afghanistan	(1971)
Angola	(1994)
Bangladesh	(1975)
Benin	(1971)
Bhutan	(1971)
Burkina Faso	(1971)
Burundi	(1971)
Central Africa Republic	(1975)
Chad	(1971)
Comoros	(1977)
Congo (Democratic Republic)	(1991)
Djibouti	(1982)
Eritrea	(1994)
Ethiopia	(1971)
Gambia	(1975)
Guinea	(1971)
Guinea-Bissau	(1981)
Haiti	(1971)
Kiribati	(1986)
Lao People's Democratic Republic	(1971)
Lesotho	(1971)
Liberia	(1990)
Madagascar	(1991)
Malawi	(1971)
Mali	(1971)
Mauritania	(1986)
Mozambique	(1988)
Myanmar	(1987)
Nepal	(1971)
Niger	(1971)
Rwanda	(1971)
Sao Tome and Principe	(1982)

Senegal	(2000)
Sierra Leone	(1982)
Solomon Islands	(1991)
Somalia	(1971)
South Sudan	(2012)
Sudan	(1971)
Tanzania	(1971)
Timor-Leste	(2003)
Togo	(1982)
Tuvalu	(1982)
Uganda	(1971)
Vanuatu	(1985)
Yemen	(1971)
Zambia	(1991)

[Source: UN Committee for Development Policy]

Are all LDCs low-income countries (LICs)?

Although the majority of current LDCs (40 of them) are low-income countries with a per-capita income of less than $1,036 (as of 2020), some of them are not because the LDC classification is also based on human development index and economic vulnerability criteria. Bangladesh, Bhutan, Myanmar, Sao Tome and Principe, Timor-Leste, and Vanuatu (which is scheduled to graduate this year – 2020) are lower-middle-income countries with per-capita income from $1,036 to $4,045; and Tuvalu is an upper-middle-income country. The per capita income for the latter group varies from $4,046 to $12,535. Crawfurd (2016) argues that the rationale for the classification of those countries as LDCs is partly to help out small and vulnerable island states.

What is the current socio-economic situation of the LDCs?

An estimated 1.06 billion people live in the world's 47 LDCs, and by 2030 over 15% of humanity will be living in them; and despite their large demographic weight, LDCs account for less than 1.5% of global GDP (UNCTAD 2020, November 12). In 2019, adds UNCTAD, the average GDP per capita in LDCs was only $991 compared with a world average of $11,069. Furthermore, the number of people living in extreme poverty in these countries has virtually stalled at nearly 36% over the past ten years; they account for 53% of people living on less than $1.90 per day and nearly 40% of humans who live on less than $3.20 a day (UNCTAD 2020).

7.2. Export Specialization

UNCTAD has classified the LDCs into six export specialization categories, based on which type of exports accounted for at least 45 percent of total exports of goods and services in 2009-2011. It has, however, used a threshold of 40 percent for five of these countries instead of 45: Bhutan, Madagascar, Mozambique, Sierra Leone, and Uganda.

Table 4: Export Specialization

Category	Country/Exporter
Agricultural & Food Exporters	Benin, Burkina Faso, Guinea-Bissau, Kiribati, Malawi, Solomon Island, Somalia, Uganda;
Fuel Exporters	Angola, Chad, Sudan, Yemen;
Manufacturers	Bangladesh, Bhutan, Cambodia, Haiti, Lesotho;
Mineral Exporters	Congo (Dem. Rep.), Guinea, Mali, Mauritania, Mozambique, Sierra Leone, Zambia;
Mixed Exporters	Afghanistan, Burundi, Central African Republic Lao (People's Dem. Rep.), Myanmar, Niger, Senegal, Togo, Tanzania;
Services Exporters	Comoros, Djibouti, Eritrea, Ethiopia, Gambia, Liberia, Madagascar, Nepal, Rwanda, Samoa, Sao Tome & Principe, Timor-Leste, Tuvalu, Vanuatu*.

[Source: UNCTAD]

This table is provided for an analytical purpose later on.

*Vanuatu is projected to graduate this year (2020).

7.3. Fragile and Conflict-Affected States (FCAS)

This study has previously identified some of the reasons that make the LDCs different from the other developing countries (ODCs). The LDCs also differ from each other in terms of some characteristics. The World Bank Group has sub-classified 25 of the 47 LDCs either as "fragile states" or "conflict-affected states," based on the nature and severity of obstacles they face. Thirteen of them are categorized as countries with "high institutional and social fragility"; ten of them as countries with "medium-intensity conflict"; and two of them as countries with "high-intensity conflict." Although this text only mentions the LDCs classified as FCAS, they are some non-LDCs that are also classified as FCAS. The World Bank Group releases an updated list of fragile and conflict states every year.

According to some analysts, fragile states (also known as weak states) usually fail to meet three key needs of their citizens, termed gaps: (i) *security gap*, meaning that the state fails to adequately protect its citizens; (ii) *capacity gap*, meaning that the state does not fully provide adequate services to its citizens, and (iii) *legitimacy gap,* meaning that the authority of the state is challenged by rivals and is not fully accepted. These states are vulnerable to both internal and external shocks.

Which countries are considered "fragile"?

The World Bank Group defines *fragile countries* as those with one or more of the following: (a) the weakest institutional and policy environment, based on a revised, harmonized CPIA (Country Policy and Institutional Assessment) score…that is below 3.0; **or** (b) the presence of a UN peacekeeping operation because this reflects a decision by the international community that a significant investment is needed to maintain peace and stability there; **or** (c) flight across borders of 2,000 or more per 100,000 population, who are internationally regarded as refugees in need of international protection, as this signals a major political or security crisis; and those that are not in medium- or high-intensity conflict…as such countries have gone beyond fragility.

Which countries are considered "countries in conflict"?

According to the World Bank Group, *countries in conflict* are identified based on the number of conflict deaths in absolute terms and relative to their population. And they are sub-divided into two categories:

(i) *Countries in a high-intensity conflict* that are defined as those with an absolute number of conflict deaths above 250 according to ACLED (Armed Conflict Location & Event Data) and 150 according to UCDP (Uppsala Conflict Data Project); **and** a number of conflict deaths relative to the population above 10 per 100,000…reflecting widespread and intense violence across many parts of the country.

(ii) *Countries in a medium-intensity conflict* are defined as

(a) countries with lower intensity conflict **or** (b) countries with a rapid deterioration of the security situation, as measured by a lower number of conflict deaths relative to the population between 1 and 2 (ACLED) *and* 0.5 and 1 (UCDP), and the number of casualties more than doubling in the last year.

World Bank (2016) posits that fragile countries experienced below-average GDP growth, under 4 percent a year, compared with almost 6 percent in LDCs as a whole between 2000 and 2014. This economic underperformance is problematic because a growth rate of 7 percent has been usually targeted by international institutions to drive development in those countries.

7.4. Heavily Indebted Poor Countries (HIPCs)

In addition to having a precarious socio-economic situation, being classified as either "fragile states" or "conflict-affected states," the majority of the LDCs are heavily indebted. The International Monetary Fund (IMF) and the World Bank have designated them as "Heavily Indebted Poor Countries." (Some other non-LDC developing states are also designated as HIPCs). This group of designated countries (LDCs as well as non-LDCs) with high levels of poverty and "unsustainable" debt are eligible for special assistance, including debt relief for poverty reduction, from the IMF, the World Bank, and other official institutions.

Development credits have usually been provided to HIPCs on highly concessional terms. Through The Paris Club (a group of official bilateral creditors mostly from developed countries), creditors work together to alleviate the debt burden of those countries by easing repayment terms. They do so for two main reasons: (1) they recognize that "unsustainable debt" is one of the pervasive factors that contribute to poverty and worsen poverty's impact on people living in the countries struggling to survive on the extreme international poverty line; (2) it is in their best interest to provide debt relief in order to minimize their loss.

7.5. COVID-19 Pandemic and LDCs

The COVID-19 global health pandemic has worsened the already fragile socio-economic situation in LDCs. As previously indicated, it is estimated "to push an additional 88 million to 115 million people into extreme poverty in 2020, with the total rising to as many as 150 million by 2021". The vast majority of these poor individuals live in LDCs, which have been hit very hard by the decline in global trade as a result of the pandemic. Country Indicators for Foreign Policy (CIFP, 2020) contends that the COVID-19 crisis has further exacerbated the performance of the Fragile and Conflict-Affected States by further weakening their capacity for response and prevention and by delinking their economies from global financial, trade, and aid flows.

Concerning the negative impact of COVID-19 on LDCs as a group, the World Trade Organization (WTO 2020, November 11) contends that LDC merchandise exports declined by 16 percent during the first half of 2020, a decline driven by a drop in exports of fuel and mining products (26 percent) and clothing (18 percent). WTO further indicates that the LDC services sector also took a hit, with preliminary estimates suggesting a drop close to 40 percent in the first six months of 2020, a hit-driven by a slump in travel exports estimated to be nearly 60 percent during the first half of 2020.

Table 4 shows a classification of LDCs by export specialization, and most of them fall into the above-described situations. As the statistical data cited are for the first half of the year, by doubling them, we get a better understanding of the impact for the full year (assuming that the situation has not deteriorated or improved). This sharp decline in services exports triggered by the COVID-19 pandemic and its devastating impact on LDCs' economies as a group have underscored these countries' dependency on tourism, "which accounts for close to half of LDC services exports."

After providing relevant background information on and examining the prevalent socio-economic situations in the least developed countries, the next chapter will address the first two of the three questions posed at the beginning of Part Three: *what has been done to reduce the level of poverty in LDCs? And how effective or ineffective have the strategies been implemented?*

Chapter 8:
Assistance to the Least Developed Countries

I n order to help the LDCs break the vicious cycle of poverty, the international community has agreed to some *special concessions*, which include benefits in the areas of:

- *Developing financing.* International donors and financial institutions have provided grants and loans with low-interest rates to LDCs.

- *Multilateral trading system.* In terms of trade, special treatments, including preferential access for their products to the markets of more developed countries, duty-free and quota-free market access have been granted to LDCs.

- *Technical assistance.* Technical assistance has been provided to LDCs in order to help them integrate the global economy (notably trade mainstreaming).

Despite the privileges, benefits, and special treatments granted, the economic situations in the LDCs as a group have worsened instead of improving. According to UNCTAD (2016), the proportion of the global poverty in those countries has more than doubled since 1990, to over 40 percent; their share of those without access to water has also doubled to 43.5 percent in the same period; and these countries now account for the majority (53.4 percent) of the 1.1 billion people worldwide who do not have access to electricity, an increase of two thirds. The current global health pandemic (COVID-19) has further exacerbated the precarious socioeconomic situations in those countries.

The least developed countries, therefore, are left behind even though the international community had pledged to "leave no one behind." Facing this fact, the UNCTAD Secretary-General states that the LDCs are the countries where the battle for poverty eradication will be won or lost (UNCTAD, 2016). As the concept "poverty eradication" is different from that of "extreme poverty eradication," this study will instead use the concept "poverty reduction," which is more realistic and feasible.

Reflecting on the plight of the LDCs, Milanovic (2006) states that economic theory predicts that globalized markets for capital and technology will help poor people 'catch up', as poor countries take advantage of cheaper access to technologies already developed in rich countries and capital flows to the developing countries where it is more scarce. However, continues Milanovic, since the late 1970s, per capita incomes have actually diverged between countries, and overall the Least Developed Countries have not grown.

Commenting on the poor economic performance of the LDCs, Reiter and Adhikari (2016, May 27) argue that many LDCs are dependent on commodity export and, due to insufficient export diversification, are struggling significantly with the latest slump in commodity prices. It is accurate that dependence on commodity export and commodity price fluctuations have made it difficult for those countries to improve their socio-economic status, but it is worth mentioning that even when commodity prices were relatively high, that had not contributed to the removal of the overwhelming majority of LDCs from the list because of the weight of the other contributing factors.

The picture painted so far for the LDCs is indeed very somber, but it is important to acknowledge that poverty reduction is a complex and multifaceted issue, and the causes are numerous. As elucidated in the previous sections, natural disasters (aggravated by climate change), inability to compete in global markets and attract private foreign investment, low savings and slow growth, corruption, and ineffective policies/strategies (both national and international) have complicated the socio-economic situation in these vulnerable countries.

Almost all the strategies used so far to promote economic development and alleviate poverty in the LDCs have failed. This study will examine three of the strategies pursued: Family Planning, Poverty Reduction Strategy (PRS) Initiative, and Heavily Indebted Poor Countries (HIPC) initiative.

8.1. Family Planning

The United Nations Population Fund (UNFPA, 2017) defines family planning as the information, means, and methods that allow individuals to decide if and when to have children, and this includes a wide range of contraceptives. UNFPA argues that when women and couples are empowered to plan whether and when to have children, women are better enabled to complete their education, increase their autonomy within their households, and improve their earning power. It also contends that access to contraceptive information is central to achieving gender equality.

In addition to the above benefits, UNFPA also contends that family planning brings "clear economic benefits." For every additional dollar that is invested in contraception, the cost of pregnancy-related care will be reduced by about three dollars, and achieving universal access to quality sexual and reproductive health services is estimated to yield returns of $120 for every dollar invested, argues UNFPA.

Because of the potential benefits, UNFPA and many other institutions support family planning as a strategy to control the number of births in LDCs, which would eventually reduce the level of poverty in those countries. However, despite all the enumerated benefits - which include the ability to limit the number of children, to control pregnancy timing (also known as *spacing children*), to reduce teenage birth rates, and to avoid unintended pregnancies – this strategy has not been successful in poor developing countries because most women do not use contraceptives.

In its attempt to explain the failure of family planning in developing countries, particularly the low-income ones, UNFPA has provided several reasons, which include (1) logistical problems such as traveling to health facilities; (2) supplies running out at health clinics; (3) social barriers such as opposition by partners, families or communities; (4) lack of knowledge about the availability of contraceptives; and (5) incorrect perception about the health risks of modern methods.

Although the reasons enumerated by UNFPA may have played an important role in the refusal of women in poor countries to use contraceptives, the fundamental one (which is omitted) is *economical*, meaning the absence of a safety net for individuals in their old age. To help understand the significance of this crucial reason, the author of this study reproduces as *Box 1* some personal conversations that he had many years ago with some women in a developing country.

Box 1. Observation on the Use of Contraceptives

When I was living in a developing country many years ago, I personally witnessed conversations among men and women on the idea of taking contraceptive measures to limit the number of children they would have. The women (in the group) opposed the use of contraceptives for a very pragmatic reason, which is purely economic. Their rationale was as follows:

Children represent a guarantee that someone will be there to take care of them personally and financially in their old age (their safety net). As the vast majority of governments in the developing world do not provide (or are unable to) any safety net, the elders have to rely on their children. When asked why they gave birth to a lot of children (instead of one or two), their response was *"one eye is no eye,"* meaning that they had to have many children. Their rationale was that some of the children might die or might not be good providers. They also argued that some of the children might have limited means or do not care. They believe that if they have several children, at least one of them will be a good provider. Some women had even expressed a preference for girls by saying: *"girls will always take care of mommy."* According to them, boys will be more attached to their wives after they get married.

The issues raised in Box 1 are very real and critical in the least developed countries. They must not be dismissed because they reflect the participants' life experiences. For instance, although global maternal mortality has declined, in low-income countries, more than half the population dies from communicable diseases or maternal, prenatal, or nutrition conditions, according to World Bank (2016). With regard to the issue of lack of social safety net, World Bank (2016) indicates that average social assistance cash benefits account for only 10 percent of poor's consumption in low-income countries. In most LDCs, people have not received any social assistance at all.

Based on people's reality described in Box 1, the rationale for the refusal to use contraceptives is obvious, and the decision to have many children is an economic one. It is therefore not practical nor advisable to take away something from someone (safety net in this case) without first replacing it with something else. The family planning strategy will most likely continue to fail until some social safety net is provided to individuals or good-paying jobs are created, which would enable people to save and have some financial security in their old age.

The above observation on family planning should be viewed as an example to in part explain the importance of using policies/strategies that are applicable and appropriate to cases in specific countries if we want to foster economic growth and development that would reduce the level of poverty in LDCs. "One size does not fit all."

8.2. Poverty Reduction Strategy (PRS) Initiative

"When a substantial proportion of a population is poor, it makes little sense to detach poverty from the dynamics of development" (United Nations Institute for Research and Development - UNIRSD, 2010).

Aware of the importance of poverty reduction in the development process and the fact that "Shareholder groups were disappointed by the poverty reduction impact of past development assistance, particularly the poor results in low-income countries," the World Bank, in conjunction with other international institutions, launched the Poverty Reduction Strategy (PRS) Initiative in 1999.

What has been the objective of the Poverty Reduction Strategy?

When the World Bank and International Monetary Fund launched the Poverty Reduction Strategy (PRS) Initiative in 1999, the objective was to signal a new way for the international donor community to "assist low-income countries in developing and implementing more effective strategies to fight poverty by supporting and sustaining a country-driven Poverty Reduction Strategy process." According to the World Bank, this new PRS process should follow **five underlying principles**:

- *Country-driven,* meaning that country ownership of the strategy should involve broad-based participation of civil society

- *Comprehensive* in recognizing the multi-dimensional nature of poverty

- *Results-oriented* and focused on outcomes that benefit the poor

- *Partnership-oriented,* involving coordinated participation of development partners such as the government, domestic stakeholders, and external donors

- Based on a *long-term perspective* for poverty reduction.

The PRS **process** also requires countries to prepare Poverty Reduction Strategy Papers (PRSPs) and their *endorsements* by the Board of the Bretton Woods Institutions (BWIs) (meaning the World

Bank and IMF) as a condition for debt relief through the Heavily Indebted Poor Country (HIPC) initiative and other monetary aid. (More on HIPC in the next section). In other words, the PRSPs are prepared by member countries in consultation with and approval by stakeholders and development partners, particularly the IMF and the World Bank.

What is the purpose of the PRSPs?

The Poverty Reduction Strategy Papers describe the country's macroeconomic, structural, and social policies in support of growth and poverty reduction, as well as associated external financing needs and major sources of financing; the PRSP was introduced to the PRS process…with a view to giving a more central role to poverty reduction and pro-poor growth considerations in the design of IMF-supported programs in low-income countries (IMF 2008, July).

What is the rationale behind the new PRS initiative?

The main goal of the new Initiative was to create a more broadly poverty-focused government. Before the adoption of the Initiative, the issue of poverty reduction was a concern confined within governments of developing countries. The PRS process (which is a response to demands from donors to show results) broadens the sphere of the poverty issue by encouraging more participation from the population, particularly the civil society, in order to increase "the influence of stakeholders in policy creation, program implementation, resource allocation, and priority settings." The PRS process encourages governments to take leadership and ownership by allowing them to implement their own plans and to allocate the aid money in accordance with the strategies that had drawn up in their poverty reduction strategy paper (PRSP).

8.3. Evaluation of the Poverty Reduction Strategy Initiative

How effective has been the Initiative?

Several case studies had been conducted to determine the impact and success of the Poverty Reduction Strategy Initiative (PRS), and the results varied from country to country depending on various factors.

Case studies, such as "Poverty reduction strategy processes in Malawi and Zambia" by Bwalya et al. (2004), reveal some difficulties encountered by countries in implementing the PRS process. Some countries are less successful than others for several reasons, including structural, socio-cultural, economic, and political, and especially the weaknesses of domestic institutions. Some countries have had difficulties in following through with "intended policies" – designed by or with the assistance of international institutions – which prevented them from achieving the desired outcomes.

8.3.1. Assessment of Malawi's and Zambia's Cases

Bwalya et al.'s report discuss the participatory aspects of the Poverty Reduction Strategy Papers (PRSPs) in **Malawi** and **Zambia**. The authors focused on the process because it "aims to include a wide range of stakeholders' views on priority setting, resource allocation and access to public goods and services." Their findings reveal that participation of development partners was significant in both countries, especially by civil society organizations, but key political institutions were marginalized. The report also indicates that the new *conditionality* – preparation of PRSP as a condition for eligibility to debt relief – puts far more emphasis on process and 'national ownership' than expected outcome indicators. Bwalya & al. also point out in their report what they consider an inherent contradiction in the PRS process by stating that:

'national ownership' is a double-edged sword. It is presumed to enhance implementation precisely because it is embedded in the existing institutional structure and culture rather than

being an imposition from abroad. However, this embedded 'national ownership' may act to conserve the retrogressive institutions that produced poverty in the first place, and this is considered anathema to poverty reduction in the contemporary situation."

Bwalya et al. have used the specific case of **Malawi** to in part render their position on the PRS process. They state that Malawi has been *good at producing impressive policy documents but extremely poor at implementing them* (emphasis), presumably owing to institutional shortcomings, including the power relationship in which they are embedded.

8.3.2. World Bank's Assessment of the PRS process

A World Bank's Independent Evaluation Group (IEG) conducted an assessment of the PRS initiative in 2004 (reproduced in "Evaluation of Poverty Reduction Support Credits" paper in June 2007) found the following:

- The PRS initiative had improved the poverty focus on national strategies and helped policymakers link sector strategies to poverty reduction;

- The initiative had added most value in countries where government leadership and the aid management process were already strong, **but** it had had less effect in countries with weak public sector capacity or donor-dominated aid relationship;

- External partners were found to have supported the PRS process **but** do not have systematically adapted the content of their assistance programs in a coordinated manner around the content of PRSs;

- The PRSs needed stronger analytical underpinnings to ensure that the poverty impact of pursued policies and programs was adequately assessed.

Aware of the *ineffectiveness* of the PRS initiative to significantly reduce the level of poverty in the least developed countries, the World Bank's IEG Evaluation (2004) made two main recommendations:

(i)   The World Bank actively promote the tailoring of PRSs to country conditions and help countries sharpen the PRSs' results focus

(ii) The World Bank help countries build the analytical capacity to determine how development programs and policies can lead to poverty reduction and that it facilitates the use of the PRS as a partnership framework.

The PRS Initiative has not been successful in significantly reducing the level of poverty in LDCs, and has not helped the majority of them to graduate from the LDC group.

How to explain the failure of reducing poverty in LDCs?

In addition to the explanations provided by Milanovic, Bwalya, et al., and the author of this study, Easterly (2006), argues that international institutions fail because aid agencies face poor incentives to deliver results and underinvest in enforcing aid conditions and performing scientific evaluations. He further argues that the system keeps going back to the same failed ideas that prevent most aid money from actually reaching the world's poor. To this observation, it is important to add embedded corruption (among other factors) as a major national impediment to poverty reduction and development

Having examined the Family Planning strategy and the Poverty Reduction Strategy, let us turn now to the Heavily Indebted Poor Country strategy.

8.4. Heavily Indebted Poor Country (HIPC) Initiative

The *Heavily Indebted Poor Country* (HIPC) initiative refers to a program launched by the World Bank and the International Monetary Fund (IMF) in 1996. To help more countries qualify for the program, an *enhanced* HIPC Initiative, which lowered the criteria for eligibility, was formed in 1999.The program was designed to ensure that the poorest countries in the world are not overwhelmed by unmanageable or unsustainable debt burdens (World Bank 2018, January 11).

What is the main purpose of the HIPC Initiative?

The HIPC Initiative is meant to provide heavily indebted poor countries with a way to permanently escape unsustainable debt burdens and transition smoothly to more normal relationships with external creditors (IMF, 2001). According to IMF, these are essential conditions for *securing the necessary financing* for sustainable growth and development and enduring poverty reduction in these countries.

When does a country achieve external debt sustainability?

A country is considered to have achieved external debt sustainability when it is able to make good on *all* of its external debt service payments – current and future – in full and without sacrificing economic growth; that is, a country that has reduced its debt burden to sustainable levels should not have to resort to rescheduling its debt or accumulating arrears (IMF, 2001).

Under HIPC, countries are required to establish a good record of implementing economic and social policy reform and prepare a Poverty Reduction Strategy Paper (PRSP) indicating how they will tackle poverty reduction; the funds made available by debt relief [which is considered as a form of multilateral aid] would be then channeled into poverty-reduction, typically through a Poverty Action Fund (PAF) that identifies pro-poor expenditures (UNU-WIDER, 2005).

In 2006 the *Multilateral Debt Relief Initiative* (MDRI) was launched with the goal of providing additional support to countries that participate in the HIPC Initiative. Since then, the two debt relief programs have worked conjunctly with the aim of alleviating the debt burden of the poor and highly-indebted countries. As of March 25, 2020, 36 countries have qualified for debt relief under the

HIPC Initiative and the MDRI. In order to qualify for debt relief, countries must demonstrate their ability for sound economic management through the satisfactory implementation of policy reforms over three years under IMF and World Bank programs (UNU-WIDER, 2005).

8.5. Criteria for Eligibility

To be eligible for the HIPC Initiative, the World Bank requires that a country must:

- Face unsustainable debt situation after the full application of the traditional debt relief mechanisms (such as the application of Naples terms under the Paris Club agreement);

- Be only eligible for highly concessional assistance from the International Development Assistance (IDA);
  (To be considered "poor" under the HIPC initiative, a country must be an "IDA-only" country, which means that it relies on highly concessional financing from IDA, which is a World Bank's concessional lending-arm).

- Have established a track record of reform and sound policies through IMF and World Bank-supported programs;

- Establish a track record of reform and develop a Poverty Reduction Strategy Paper (PRSP) that involves civil society participation.

The last requirement clearly shows that the international institutions have linked the two programs – The Poverty Reduction Strategy (PRS) Initiative and the Heavily Indebted Poor Country (HIPC) Initiative. In fact, the majority of countries participating in both HIPC and PRS initiatives are the same, except a few HIPCs that are not classified as LDCs even though some are LICs (low-income countries). The two initiatives are linked because "unsustainable debt" (or "debt overhang") is considered as one of the factors that contribute to poverty in a country. Because of this interconnectedness, there is a near consensus that the removal of a debt burden is a *pre-condition* for growth and sustainable development.

8.6. The HIPC Initiative Process

Without going into all the details, the Initiative involves two stages. The first stage is called the *decision point,* and the second is referred to as the *completion point.* The time that it takes a country to pass from the decision point to the completion point is called the *interim period.* According to IMF (2020, March 25), countries must meet certain criteria (as previously enumerated), commit to poverty reduction, and demonstrate a good track record over time; and once a country reaches its decision point, it may immediately begin receiving interim relief on its debt service falling due.

To reach the *decision point,* however, a country must fulfill four conditions under the HIPC Initiative assistance. One of the four conditions is the preparation of a Poverty Reduction Strategy Paper (PRSP) that lays out the actions that the country will take not only to reduce poverty but also to implement policy reform to reach the *completion point,* which allows a country to receive the full debt relief and irrevocable reduction in debt available under the HIPC Initiative, that country must meet three established criteria. One of them is the adoption and implementation of its PRSP for at least one year.

8.7. Assessment of the HIPC Initiative

How effective has been the Highly Indebted Poor Country (HIPC) Imitative?

As previously stated, a few HIPCs are low-income countries even though they are not classified as LDCs. This assessment will first focus on a case study related to three of those countries.

8.7.1. Lessons from three Latin American HIPCs

There has been a perception that Poverty Reduction Strategy (PRS) processes in Latin America and the Caribbean had not successfully engaged with political actors and institutions as per requirement. In other words, the process has not been followed as it should have been. Overseas Development Institute (ODI) was commissioned on behalf of the Latin American and Caribbean PRS Donor Network to assess the situation. ODI conducted the assessment based on experiences in three Latin American HIPCs: Bolivia, Honduras, and Nicaragua. The political nature of the endeavor did complicate the task.

ODI (2006), however, reports the following:

The PRS approach has been compromised by the fact that a single instrument – preparation of a comprehensive plan document, with broad consultation – has been made to serve different purposes. In reality, these need to be met in different ways. As a consequence, *it has served none particularly well* (emphasis), although some better than others. The function it has performed *least well is that of getting genuine political buy-in to poverty reduction as an objective* (emphasis). A coordinated multi-pronged approach is a key to a more satisfactory relationship between political systems, donor actors, and PRSs.

The above assessment indicates that both the PRS and the HIPC failed to achieve the ultimate goal of *poverty reduction* because politicians in the three countries did not "buy-in to poverty reduction as an objective." This revelation is a testimony that poverty alleviation will not occur in a country without the *political will and commitment* of the governing authorities.

The assessment, being both a political and technical document, has many nuances, some more complex than others. Therefore, interested readers should refer to the full document (see References).

In its attempt to address this delicate political situation, ODI (2006) made several recommendations. Among them are:

- The overarching recommendation is that agencies should, individually and collectively, get into the habit of thinking about carrying forward the PRS *approach* in a country rather than carrying forward the PRS. The way forward is a more differentiated method of working, one that recognizes that political goals have to be attained politically and technical ones technically.

- Assisting the emergence of country ownership by engaging on political terrain on the basis of a solid understanding of long-term processes of change;

- Accepting new flexibility of approach in pursuing systems alignments and aid harmonization;

- While facing agreements, such as those for budget support, to focus selectively on short-term policy actions that are both useful and likely to be taken, given known political commitments.

In addition to the above, ODI (2006) made another recommendation (among many others) that is very revealing. It states:

We recommend a judicious combination of informal, behind-the-scenes interaction with politicians with regular signed contributions to national debate (e.g., in newspaper columns) and occasional well-prepared, formal public position statements. Development cooperation agencies have a *duty* (emphasis) to do whatever part they can in ensuring that the overall incentive structure remains *favorable to democracy and does not force Latin American politicians into blind alleys* (emphasis), as has happened with damaging consequences for the region as a whole in various past periods. It is, however, essential that this is informed by a deep understanding of the relevant issues, *not ideological knee-jerks* (emphasis).

The above citations reveal the intricacy and complexity of the issue of poverty reduction, which is more political than technical/financial. In fact, the ODI's paper is entitled "Politics and Poverty Reduction Strategies: Lessons from Latin American HIPCs." In order to remain objective, the author of this study has provided citations to enable the readers to draw their own conclusion. The analysis of Latin America's case has led the author of this research study to make two important observations:

(i) To effectively address poverty reduction in low-income countries (LICs), three basic requirements must converge; political will, political commitment, and resources.

The first two requirements are within the control of a nation-state, but the third one requires the assistance of the international community because LICs lack the necessary resources to successfully deal with this issue; thus the importance of national and international cooperation.

(ii) A bridge between *principles* (in this case, PRS standards) and *feasibility* (in this case, the political reality in a specific country) must be built.

As a response to the question posed earlier: *How effective has been the HIPC initiative?* The consensus is that the Initiative has several shortcomings:

(1) The criteria for eligibility were too complex and restrictive. As a result, several poor and highly indebted countries were unable to meet them;

(2) The HIPC process was too slow.

In this regard, Isar (2012) contends that countries such as Bolivia, Mauritania, and Uganda had to wait for months until their creditors distributed the relief funds. In the same vein, UNU-WIDER (2005) states that the inherent defect with the HIPC approach is that the resources to fund pro-poor expenditures are not released until the end of the process. UNU-WIDER also asserts that if the primary objective is poverty reduction, priority should be given to 'pro-poor expenditures' over 'pro-poor policies,' but the current approach to HIPC conditionality reverses these priorities.

Although the argument of releasing the funds before the end of the process makes sense, it is critical to ascertain that the funds are not misused, which has often been the case. In this context, Hall, Karakas & Schlosky (2016) cites the case of Nigeria in which the country's President, a large foreign aid recipient, reportedly spent $1 million of poverty alleviation funds to sponsor two U.S popular music artists to perform at a music festival in 2006; and in February 2013, continue the authors, Nigeria spent another $500,000 inviting a U. S celebrity to co-host an event called *Love Like A Movie*. It is obvious that these events have nothing to do with *poverty reduction*, which has been the main purpose of the debt relief funds. In this case, the mismatch between the donors' intent and the recipient's utilization of the funds illustrates how aid can serve as a perverse incentive.

(3) Isar (2012) argues that the HIPC ignores exogenous economic shocks that unavoidably affect many debt-burdened countries. To corroborate this position, Isar mentions the case of Uganda, where the fall of global commodity prices damaged its economy and particularly its exports, which is the main source of its foreign earnings.

In summary, Isar (2012) states that the HIPC cannot be an entirely successful initiative unless its current criteria and mechanisms are either substantially replaced or modified.

(4) Anup Shah (2001) contends that the HIPC Initiative has been met with a lot of criticism for not actually helping the countries it is supposed to be helping (the indebted nations) while helping those it wasn't necessarily meant to (the rich nations).

(5) UNCTAD 2019 (citing Ugo Panizza) reports that the Heavily Indebted Poor Countries Initiative and Multilateral Debt Relief Initiative were supposed to put an end to the debt sustainability problems of low-income countries; clearly, things did not work as expected, as a substantial number of least developed countries are now classified as being in debt distress or having a high risk of debt distress.

The best and easiest way to determine whether the HIPC Initiative has been a success or not is to refer to its main purpose as previously stated, "…to provide heavily indebted poor countries with a way to *permanently* (emphasis) escape unsustainable debt burdens and transition smoothly to more normal relationships with external creditors". Has this goal been attained? Have the HIPCs achieved "external debt sustainability"?

The above UNCTAD's citation has unequivocally provided the answers. Moreover, UNCTAD asserts that LDC (the majority of low-income countries) total stock of external debt has more than doubled between 2007 and 2017, jumping from $146 billion to $313 billion.

Concluding Comments

All three of the strategies examined in this study – Family Planning, Poverty Reduction Strategy Initiative, and Heavily Indebted Poor Countries – have been very *ineffective* in attaining their ultimate objective of *reducing poverty in the least developed countries* for several and complex reasons explained in this research paper.

The first two questions posed at the beginning of chapter seven – *what has been done to help reduce the level of poverty in LDCs?* And *whether the strategies implemented have been effective or ineffective* - have been addressed. The next chapter will investigate the third question posed: *why has it been so difficult to graduate from the LDC category?*

Chapter 9:
Graduation

As previously stated, it has been very difficult for the least developed countries to exit the LDC category. Since the establishment of the list of countries designated by the United Nations as LDCs in 1971 because they "are deemed highly disadvantaged in their development process for structural, historical and also geographical reasons," only five of them have been successful in graduating from the LDC status. These countries are Botswana in 1994, Cape Verde in 2007, Maldives in 2011, Samoa in 2014, and Equatorial Guinea in 2017.

What are the factors contributing to the graduation of the above five countries?

Before discussing the requirements for graduation, this paper provides some explanations for the ability of each of the five countries to exit the LDC group. According to UNCTAD (2017), **Equatorial Guinea** was the fifth country to graduate, but the first one to do so based on the 'income only' criterion (see section 9.1); its GNI per capita - $16,089 – was almost six times the income-only graduation threshold of $2,824. Equatorial Guinea, continues UNCTAD, was able to exit the LDC group with such a relatively high level of income because of its extractive industries, which is the largest in the economy, accounting for 41 percent of GDP (together with utility industries) in 2014.

Export was another reason for graduation. In 2015 Equatorial Guinea had an export product concentration of 0.69, compared to an average for LDC of only 0.26 (UNCTAD 2017). However, this high level of export concentration could become problematic because it makes the country very vulnerable to external shocks, such as commodity prices.

In the case of **Cape Verde,** tourism, trade, foreign investment, and privatization seem to be the reasons that explain its graduation. United Nations (2008) posits that the country has pursued market-oriented and people-centered policies, private sector development, privatization, trade liberalization, and promotion of investment, particularly in tourism, transport, and telecommunication infrastructure since 1991 and, as a result, its GDP grew at impressive 6.5 percent per annual and reached US$ 1.3 billion in 2006.

Regarding the **Maldives,** tourism, fishing, foreign aid, and good governance seem to be the reasons for graduation. A document submitted by the Government of Maldives to UNCTAD in 2001 indicates that the country's economy is primarily propelled by tourism and fishing, and the tourism sector has been the engine of growth of the economy during the last decade, earning much needed foreign currency. The document also states that the tourism sector accounted for 34.5 percent of GDP during 1995-1998, with a growth rate of 7.8 percent during the same period.

Sound macroeconomic management also significantly contributes to Maldives' good economic performance. In this regard, the Maldives' document contends that the government demonstrated considerable prudence in macroeconomic management, and gross domestic savings between 1993 and 1996 were 34.8 percent of GDP, while gross domestic investment was as high as 45.6 percent during the same period. The document further indicates that foreign aid – both bilateral and multilateral – played a key role in the socio-economic development of Maldives because that aid bridged the resource gap and accelerated the development process.

In another document prepared by the Government of Maldives for the Maldives Partnership Forum (MPF) to be held in March 2009, the Government also mentioned international trade as an important factor in the country's economy. According to that document, international trade in tourism services and fisheries together accounted for 60-70% of the country's GDP. The Government indicates that all the mentioned factors have contributed to the country's graduation.

In the case of **Botswana,** https://www.bbc.co.uk/news//world-africa-13040376 points out that Botswana is the world's largest producer of diamonds, and the trade has transformed it into a middle-income nation.

Diamond trade, however, could not have been the only factor that facilitated Botswana's graduation. Other LDCs (such as Chad, the Democratic Republic of the Congo, and Guinea) have not been able to use their mineral wealth to significantly reduce poverty and exit the LDC classification. UNCTAD (2016) corroborates this view when it posits that despite macroeconomic benefits, extractive industries have contributed little to poverty reduction. *Good governance* must have also been a primordial determinant, among other factors.

In their assessment of the economic performance of Botswana, Todaro & Smith (2017) assert that Botswana shows that mineral wealth can be a benefit (instead of a curse) in a country that has the *appropriate political development* (emphasis) in place. They further point out that Botswana has experienced by far the highest rate of growth in Sub-Saharan Africa: 8.4% per year over the 1985-1990 period and a still-high 6.0% in 1990-2005. They attribute this success to the benefits of foreign direct investment, favorable geography (huge diamond deposits), and favorable institutions.

Regarding **Samoa**, diversification, tourism, offshore banking, light manufacturing, and foreign direct investment have been credited for the country's graduation. At first, the economy relied on agriculture and fishing, and then the country decided to diversify. According to https://www.bbc.co.uk/news/world/asia-15655855, attempts at diversification have been a success: tourism has grown in part because of the islands' scenic attraction and fine beaches; offshore banking services spearheads an expanding services sector, and light manufacturing has attracted foreign investment.

While this section of the study is being re-written, **Vanuatu** - a small island in the western Pacific - graduated in December 2020. For only the sixth time since the inception of the LDC status by the United Nations in 1971, a country has left the ranks of the LDCs.

Let us now turn to the criteria for graduation.

9.1. Requirements for Graduation

Every three years, the Committee for Development Policy (CDP) of the United Nations' Economic Council (ECOSOC) reviews the list of LDCs to decide which countries are qualified to be included in the LDC category or meet the criteria for graduation, which are – as previously mentioned – *per capita income, human assets, and economic vulnerability.*

How does a country qualify for graduation?

According to UNCTAD (2017), a country normally qualifies for graduation if it has met the graduation thresholds under at least two of the three criteria in at least two consecutive triennial reviews of the list. However, if the three-year average per capita GNI of an LDC has risen to a level of at least double the graduation threshold, and if this performance is considered durable, the country is deemed eligible for graduation regardless of its score under the other criteria. This rule is commonly referred to as the *'income rule'* graduation rule. This is the rule under which Equatorial Guinea graduated in 2017.

The overwhelming majority of LDCs have not been able to meet the criteria, which in part explains their inability to leave the ranks of LDC status. However, other factors are sometimes considered in exceptional cases. For instance, the Committee for Development Policy recommended the graduation of Vanuatu in 2012, but the General Assembly of the United Nations decided to delay the country's graduation to December 2020 "in recognition of the severe economic and social consequences after Tropical Cyclone Pam struck [the island] in March 2015".

The General Assembly was able to postpone the date because after a country is recommended for graduation and that the General Assembly has endorsed the recommendation, the graduating country benefits from a grace period of three years before graduation officially takes place. During that period, the graduating country continues to be an LDC. As mentioned earlier, Vanuatu did graduate in December 2020.

What is the rationale for the grace period?

The grace period is designed to enable the graduating State and its development and trading partners to agree on a 'smooth transition' strategy so that the planned loss of LDC status does not disturb the socio-economic progress of the country (UNCTAD, 2016).

9.2. The Significance of Graduation

Graduation from the LDC category is considered a significant milestone reached by an LDC in the development process, but several obstacles remain. In its assessment of the significance of leaving the LDC status, UNCTAD (2016) states the following:

- Graduation in principle marks the point at which an LDC has escaped sufficiently from the vicious cycles which obstruct its development to benefit from international markets on an equal basis with ODCs (other developing countries).

- Graduation thus marks a shift from dependency to a greater degree of self-reliance.

- Graduation is the first milestone in a marathon of development, not the winning post in a race to escape LDC status. It marks the end of a *political and administrative* but the completion of an *economic or developmental process.*

- It is not enough for LDCs to graduate; they need to achieve graduation with momentum. Laying the foundations for their subsequent development to avoid the pitfalls of the post-graduation phase.

- Graduation with momentum requires the development of productive capacities and structural transformation of the economy. This, not the fulfillment of the statistical criteria for graduation, should be the primary objective of graduation strategies.

- The economic and social divergence between LDCs and ODCs, including in productive capacities, makes the LDC category more relevant than ever.

- While the "how" of graduation is more important than the "when" economically, the reverse may be the case politically, giving rise to potential tension between the two.

9.3. Causes for Non-Graduation

As to the question of *why it has been so difficult to graduate from the LDC group,* several reasons have been given to explain the inability of LDCs to leave the category. The overriding one, of course, has been the difficulty to meet the required criteria, and some of the underlying causes identified have been the following:

- LDCs' difficulties with the implementation of 'intended policies' designed by international institutions

- Misallocation or misappropriation of budgetary funds intended to go towards poverty reduction

- The imposition of conditionalities, such as 'tied' aid

- "Poverty's historical acceptance in some parts of the world as irreversible."

- Lack of capital (human, financial and social)

- High-level of population growth in LDCs

- Low-level of production and economic growth

- Weaknesses of domestic institutions

- Natural disasters (aggravated by climate change)

- Lack of diversified export and inability to attract foreign investment.

- Poverty Trap

- "Reluctance" to Graduation

9.4. Remarks on Some of the Enumerated Causes

As this study has addressed most of the above-mentioned causes (in one form or another) in previous sections, it will briefly comment on the last three.

9.4.1. Lack of Diversified Exports

The lack of diversification has not only prevented the least developed countries from taking advantage of global trade, but it has also made them very vulnerable to global commodity prices. Exports from LDCs (as well as some ODCs) are highly concentrated and dominated by a few commodities whose prices are very volatile, depending on global economic trends. As Table 4 illustrates, LDCs are mainly agricultural and food, fuel, and mineral exporters. In 38 LDCs, says UNCTAD (2016), commodities accounted for more than two-thirds of merchandise exports in 2013-2015. This commodity dependence has not only aggravated LDCs' vulnerability to exogenous shocks but has also engendered what is referred to as a *commodity-dependence trap*.

Commenting on this *trap* triggered by trade and financial relations, UNCTAD (2016) asserts that a complex set of interrelated trade and financial relations may lock a country into a disadvantageous pattern of market integration, exposing it to boom-and-bust cycles that ultimately compound its structural vulnerabilities and *exacerbate poverty* (emphasis).

Furthermore, LDCs' reliance on few commodities for exports, combined with volatility in international commodity prices and a heavy dependence on imports of essential goods, generally results in a trade deficit, which worsens the economic situation in those countries.

9.4.2. Poverty Trap

Poverty is very pervasive in LDCs as a group, and it has been extremely difficult for them to escape because they usually fall into what is called a *poverty trap*. This situation involves a vicious cycle in which poverty and underdevelopment lead to more poverty and underdevelopment. In other words, poverty outcomes reinforce themselves and act as causes of poverty itself. For instance, "low incomes and slow growth increase poverty, while poverty slows growth by limiting investment" (UNCTAD, 2016).

Establishing linkage between *poverty trap* and *commodity dependence*, UNCTAD affirms that the international aspect of the poverty trap is particularly apparent in those countries that are heavily dependent on primary commodities.

9.4.3. "Reluctance" to Graduation

It is argued that some LDCs do not graduate because they do not want to lose the "concessions associated with LDC status," which include (as previously indicated) benefits such as grants and low-interest loans from international donors and financial institutions; preferential (duty-free) access to the markets of developed countries and special treatments; and technical assistance.

In response to the argument 'reluctance' to graduation, UNCTAD (2016) states that while some LDC governments resisted the idea of graduation during the 1990s and 2000s, many now seem to take a much more positive view, interpreting reclassification as synonymous with irreversible progress and a reflection of their proactive efforts to achieve such progress.

What happens after graduation?

As the challenges and vulnerabilities facing an LDC do not automatically disappear with graduation, a process has been put in place by the international community to support a newly graduated country in its development trajectory. This process encompasses the concept of a *smooth transition*, which "embodies the principle that LDC-specific support should be phased out in a gradual and predictable manner following graduation." The transition procedure is designed to prevent a reversion to the LDC status and not to disrupt the new graduate's progress towards sustainable development.

The process also includes some post-graduation procedures, which are according to UNCTAD:

(1) The graduated country reports annually to the UN Committee for Policy Development (CDP) on the implementation of the smooth transition strategy for three years;

(2) CDP monitors development progress in consultation with the graduated country for three years and reports to ECOSOC (UN Economic and Social Council, which oversees CDP);

(3) The graduated country reports to the CDP as a *complement to two triennial* reviews on implementation of the smooth transition strategy;

(4) CDP monitors development progress in consultation with the graduated country as a complement to two triennial reviews and reports results to ECOSOC.

The above procedures are designed "to provide assurances to LDCs that the international community will ensure that the continued development progress is a shared objective, and that assistance to the country will not be withdrawn in a manner that is inconsistent with that objective" (CDP 2012, cited by UNCTAD, 2016).

Concluding Remarks

The analysis of the sections on enumerated causes for non-graduation, the significance of graduation, the path to graduation, among other factors, explain the reasons why it has been so difficult for countries classified as LDCs to leave the LDC status. It also explains why *only* six countries (including the recent graduation of Vanuatu) have exited the LDC category since 1971.

General Conclusion

Part one of this study has introduced the issue of *Global Economic Inequality* by examining income and wealth inequality within and across countries. It has also investigated the causes and consequences of inequality (which are numerous and complex) and evaluated several proposals to mitigate the negative impacts of this enduring issue.

The study has found that economic inequality has increased in nearly all regions of the world in recent decades; the economic gap between the rich and the poor has widened across the globe; the world's richest one percent (1%) hold over 50 percent of the world's wealth and 62 billionaires own the same amount of wealth as 3.5 billion people who make up the poorest half of the world's population.

The study has also found that wealth inequality has risen at different speeds in different countries or regions. For instance, in the United States, the top 1% wealth share rose from 22% to 39% in 2014, while the increase in top-wealth shares in France and the United Kingdom was more moderate over the past forty years. In China and Russia, the top 1% wealth share doubled between 1995 and 2015 from 15% to 30% and from 22% to 43%, respectively.

Regarding wealth inequality in the United States, the study has revealed that for the first time in U.S. history, the top twelve (12) U.S. billionaires surpassed a combined wealth of $1 trillion as of August 13, 2020.

The study has also found a strong linkage between inequality and poverty. They are two different issues, and that a high level of economic inequality is usually manifested in high levels of poverty in some groups of individuals and countries, especially in the least developed countries.

After evaluating several proposed solutions to economic inequality, six policy areas, according to the World Bank, have proved to be effective in reducing inequality because they offer very few trade-offs between efficiency and equity and have worked repeatedly in different settings around the world. The six policy areas are: (1) early childhood development and nutrition interventions; (2) universal health coverage; (3) universal access to quality education; (4) cash transfers to poor families; (5) rural infrastructure – especially roads and electrification; and (6) progressive taxation.

The study has also revealed that the current public health and economic crises generated by the coronavirus pandemic (COVID-19) have further widened the economic inequality gaps between the 'haves' and the 'have-nots.' While these dual crises have had adverse impacts on low-income workers around the world, the fortunes of billionaires have expanded. The combined wealth of all U.S. billionaires, for example, have increased by $821 billion (28 percent) between March 28, 2020, and September 10, 2020, from approximately $2.947 trillion to $3.768 trillion.

Part two of the study has addressed the issue of *global Poverty*. After explaining the different concepts of poverty and how they are measured, the study has considered the state of poverty around the world, identified and examined some of the causes and consequences of poverty, and identified and evaluated some of the proposals to combat poverty around the world.

This part of the study has found that 55% of the world population have no access to social protection, more than 736 million lived below the international poverty line ($1.90 a day) in 2015, and around 10 percent of the world population is living in *extreme poverty* and struggling to fulfill the most basic needs like health, education, and access to water and sanitation; most of the people living below the international poverty line belong to two regions of the world: Southern Asia and Sub-Saharan Africa. In higher poverty lines, 24.1 percent of the world lived on less than $3.20 a day, and 43.6 percent on less than $5.50 a day in 2017.

The study has also revealed that in 2018 half of the poor are children, about 70 percent of the global poor aged 15 and over have no schooling or only some basic education and that women represent a majority of the poor in most regions. Global extreme poverty is expected to rise for the first time in over 20 years as the COVID-19 pandemic is expected to push an additional 88 million to 115 million people into extreme poverty, bringing the total between 703 and 729 million.

The study has further revealed that despite the overall wealth of the European Union, poverty in the EU is still at a relatively high level and rapidly increasing, with 17.3% of the EU-28 population, more than 118 million people or 23.5% of the EU-

28 population at risk of poverty or social exclusion, 7.5% is severely materially deprived, and 10.5% is living in households with very low work intensity.

The study has also found that in the United States, 38.1 million lived in poverty, which means that those making less than the Federal government's official poverty rate represented 11.85% of the population in 2018. Furthermore, 5.3% of the population – or 17.3 million people – live in *deep poverty,* with incomes below 50% of their poverty thresholds, and 29.9% of the population – or 93.6 million people – live close to poverty, with incomes less than two times that of their poverty thresholds.

Part three of the study has considered the issue of poverty reduction within a specific group of 47 countries designated by the United Nations as the *Least Developed Countries* (LDCs) as of 2019. Of these countries, 21 of them have been on the LDC list since the inception of the category in1971, and only five of them have been successful in leaving the LDC status. This part of the study has (1) investigated what has been done to help reduce the level of poverty in LDCs; (2) examined the effectiveness or ineffectiveness of the strategies implemented; and (3) sought to determine why it has been so difficult to graduate from the LDC category.

After identifying the main features of LDCs and the required criteria for countries to be classified as such, the study has investigated the assistance provided to *least developed countries* in order to help them break the vicious circle of poverty. The study has found that some *special concessions* have been granted to support this group of countries. These concessions include the following benefits:

(1) International donors and financial institutions have provided grants and loans with low-interest rates to LDCs;

(2) In terms of trade, special treatments, including preferential access for their products to the markets of more developed countries, have been granted;

(3) Technical assistance has been provided to LDCs in order to help them integrate the global economy (notably trade mainstreaming).

Towards the attainment of the desired goal – poverty reduction - several strategies, which include *Family Planning, Poverty Reduction Strategy (PRS) Initiative,* and *Heavily Indebted Poor Countries* (HIPC)

Initiative, were implemented. Despite the special concessions granted and several development strategies pursued, the study has found that the economic situations in the least developed countries as a group have worsened instead of improving. They have fallen further behind the rest of the world in terms of economic development.

The proportion of global poverty in LDCs has more than doubled since 1990 to over 40 percent; their share of those without access to water has also doubled to 43.5 percent in the same period; and these countries now account for the majority (53.4 percent) of the 1.1 billion people worldwide who do not have access to electricity, an increase of two thirds (UNCTAD, 2016).

As to why it has been so difficult for the least developed countries to leave the LDC status, the study has revealed numerous causes, which include (1) LDCs' difficulties with the implementation of 'intended policies' designed by international institutions; (2) misallocation or misappropriation of budgetary funds intended to go towards poverty reduction; (3) imposition of 'conditionalities,' such as 'tied' aid; (4) lack of capital (human, financial and social); (5) high-level of the population in LDCs; (5) low-level of production and economic growth; (6)

weaknesses of domestic institutions; (7) natural disasters (aggravated by climate change; (8) lack of diversified export, and inability to attract foreign investment.

Appendices

The following articles were originally published on *LinkedIn.com*. As this book refers to them, the author reprints them as Appendix I and Appendix II for the convenience of the readers.

Appendix I:

GLOBALIZATION AT A CROSSROADS

By *JClaude Germain, Ph.D.*

(First published on June 25, 2020)

The world economies have undergone profound changes since the 1980s and 1990s and more so since the collapse of the Soviet Union block and the establishment of the World Trade Organization (WTO) in 1995 in replacement of the General Agreements on Tariffs and Trade (GATT). This is considered as the *third wave* of globalization, meaning the integration of world economies into one global economy/market, as per economists' viewpoint. However, events such as the 2007-2008 global financial crisis, trade conflicts among large countries – especially the ongoing tensions between the United States and China - and COVID-19 (coronavirus disease 2019) have shaken the foundation of globalization. As a result, several observers and analysts have questioned its future. The influential magazine *The Economist* titled the cover of its May 16th – 22nd issue *"Goodbye globalisation"* even though it does not wish this outcome.

Is globalization "dead"? *Not so fast.*

As globalization is not a new phenomenon and went through challenges before, let us examine what history has taught us. After 'World War I' ended the *first wave of globalization* (1870-1914), which was put in motion by decreases in tariff barriers and development technologies such as horsepower, steamships, and railroads, governments – especially during the Great Depression in the 1930s – reverted to protectionism. They imposed tariffs on imported goods in an attempt to protect their domestic markets. This practice resulted in a decline in international trade, approximately 5% of exports as a share of world income.

After World War II, internationalism prevailed over nationalism, and the *second wave of globalization* (1945-1980) emerged because the experience with protectionism was harmful to world trade. During the second wave, governments lowered trade barriers again, which increased per capita incomes within industrialized countries.

Manufactured products were mostly freed of trade barriers among developed countries, but products from developing countries did not have free access to markets of industrialized countries. Barriers were removed for only agricultural products that did not compete with agricultural products in industrialized nations. Most barriers remained in place for manufactured products originated from the developing world.

As the developing countries did not benefit from the growth of trade in manufacturing and services and were dissatisfied with the global trade system, they asked for better access to markets of the industrialized countries. This latter group of countries also wanted to expand their markets and have more access to worldwide resources. This combination of interests led to the third wave of globalization.

The *third wave of globalization* (1980 to present) has been a significant improvement over the second for several reasons. First, industrialized countries further lowered or removed some barriers such as tariffs and exchange controls in international trade and finance; second, factors such as rapid changes in technology and communications, economic incentives, and reduction in the costs of transportation have facilitated trade liberalization and globalization; third, the establishment of the WTO as a rules-based organization 'ensures that trade flows as predictably and freely as possible'; fourth, developing countries cut tariffs and opened their markets to foreign competition; fifth, the pace of global integration – the widening and intensifying of links between high-income and developing countries – have accelerated.

The above developments have created a growing interdependence of countries that resulted in increasing integration of trade, finance, people, and ideas. These changes have made it possible for some developing countries, particularly the emerging economies such as Brazil, China, and India, to break into the markets for manufactured goods of the industrialized countries. Other developing countries such as Bangladesh, Indonesia, Malaysia, Mexico, Thailand, and Turkey have successfully used their competitive advantage in labor-intensive manufacturing to benefit from this third wave of globalization. In the process, China became the world's powerhouse for manufacturing.

What has ensued?

Globalization has not worked well for all and has contributed to global inequality. As many developing countries had been left behind and marginalized, they complained about the unevenness of globalization globalization, but their complaints were largely ignored. More globalization was the prescribed remedy, meaning they had to open their economies more to the outside world.

However, the attitude changed when people from industrialized countries began to complain about the negative effects of globalization on their livelihoods. In response to increasing manufactured goods exports from some developing/emerging economies, the industrialized world adopted protectionist measures. They stopped prescribing *more openness* as a remedy and threw sand into the wheels of globalization instead.

In addition to protectionist trade policies, the United States and European countries tightened their immigration policies in an attempt to shield their labor markets. That created a dilemma for the business community. By limiting the number of foreign migrants, governments make it harder for businesses to reduce their labor costs, which is a significant share of their total costs.

How to deal with this dilemma?

To circumvent restrictions on international labor mobility, transnational firms have used various arrangements that amount to labor mobility without migration. One of these arrangements is *offshore outsourcing*, and *global value chains* became key aspects of globalization. That created a different problem for industrialized countries because their own workers started complaining by saying, "our jobs went overseas, and that is unfair to us."

What to do?

The third wave is still on-going, but the future of globalization is in doubt because *nationalism, trade tensions,* and presently COVID-19 have struck severe blows to trade liberalization. Furthermore, many workers in industrialized countries who lost their jobs in the process have blamed globalization, although more jobs have been lost to automation/technologies, and the WTO's rules have been challenged. More restrictions on the movement of people, goods, and capital and talks about repatriation (reshoring) of supply chains have further clouded the future of globalization.

As I have mentioned in my article "Integration of World Economies," dated November 30, 2018, and published on LinkedIn.com, revisiting the concept of globalization is a necessary step to take at this juncture in order to make it more inclusive and equitable; it has left too many countries and people behind, particularly the most vulnerable ones. However, the announcement of its death is *premature.* The interconnectedness of people/countries and the complexity of global markets are difficult to disentangle. Protectionism, import-substitution, and autarky (self-sufficiency) were already practiced and abandoned. Although there will always be winners and losers, globalization needs to be transformed/improved to mitigate its negative effects *but* not discarded.

Because of *rapport de force* – meaning the influence and efficacy of the entities involved – some powerful nation-states are tempted to favor *bilateralism* over *multilateralism* for short-term gains, but this approach will bring more resentments in the long term because it is detrimental to less-powerful nation-states and consumers in general in terms of costs. Multilateralism in the form of rules-based institutions is more palatable because it mitigates some of the negative effects of *rapport de force.*

Appendix II:

COVID-19: "THE CHICKEN OR THE EGG" DILEMMA

By JClaude Germain, Ph.D.

(First published on November 30, 2020)

The COVID-19 pandemic has had a devastating impact on the global economy and people (more severe in some countries than others). It has forced government officials, policymakers, health professionals, and economics professionals to face and deal with the age-old dilemma of which came first *"the chicken or the egg?"* (**Health or the economy** in this case).

Should governments pursue policies to stabilize (or stimulate) the economy first or combat the pandemic first?

In their attempt to address the dilemma, governments have imposed restrictions on the movement of people in the forms of lockdowns, physical (social) distancing, and limited air traveling; they have also curtailed the operations of several businesses. After witnessing the devastating impact of these measures on the economy (particularly the restaurant, and tourism, and hospitality industries), governments have relaxed the restrictions and allowed some businesses to re-open and resume operations in order to mitigate the negative effects on workers and businesses.

The relaxation of the restrictions and re-opening of businesses have generated an accelerating surge, with more people tested positive for the virus and hospitalized, and businesses forced to close again.

Thus the dilemma remains: *which comes first, health or the economy?*

In addition to the above dilemma, COVID-19 (1) reveals the interconnectedness of the various dimensions of globalization (political, economic, socio-cultural, and ecological); (2) proves that globalization is difficult to circumvent because no country is isolated and can unilaterally and successfully address global phenomena, including epidemics, climate change, cross-country crimes, and violence; (3) underscores the importance of global co-operation and multilateral institutions. The legitimacy of these institutions, however, depends on their relevance to the welfare of the global society via national governments.

Due to the multi-faceted nature of globalization and the fact that an economy operates within a socio-cultural milieu and a geopolitical context, it might be time to use a broader and more integrated approach to globalization, which would encompass aspects other than trade, finance, and investment in economic analysis and practice. This integrated approach would use a broader definition, such as "globalization is the integration of trade, finance, investment, people, ideas, and the rapid proliferation of communication and information technology." This change in approach, of course, would make the economists' task more complex because it requires the use of an integrated methodology (a combination of quantitative and qualitative methods) in order to measure/analyze variables that are difficult to quantify.

References

America-The Jesuit Review (2018, February 22). "Are NGOs in Haiti doing more harm than good?" Retrieved from https://www.americamagazine.org/politics-siciety/2818/02/22/are-mgos-haiti/doing-more-harm-good.

An Approach Paper. Retrieved from www.ieg.worldbankgroup.org/sites/default/files/ Data...

Banerjee, A.V. & Duflo, E. (2019). *Good Economics for Hard Times.* India: Thomson Press India Ltd.

Bwalya, E., Rakner, L., Svasand, L., Tostensen, A., & Tsoka, M. (2004). Poverty Reduction Strategy Processes in Malawi and Zambia. Norway: Chr. Michelson Institute. Retrieved from http://cmi.no/publications

CASE at LSE (2018). "How are Inequality and Poverty Linked?"

Causes, Consequences, and Reform. New York: Cambridge University Press.

CIFP (2020, September 8). Fragile and Conflict-Affected States in the Age of COVID-19. Retrieved from www.carleton.ca/cifp

Collier, P. (2007). *The Bottom Billion: Why the Poorest Countries Are*

Concern Worldwide USA (2020, 4 March). (11 Top Causes of Global". Retrieved from: https://www.concernusa.org/story/causes-of-poverty/

Context of Globalization". Retrieved from www.fao.org/sd.

Crawfurd, L. (2016, December 16). Beyond Brexit: When are the Least-Developed Countries Not the Least Developed? Center for Global Development. Retrieved from https://www.cgdev.org/blog/beyond-brexit-when-are-least-developed-countries-not-least-developed.

Docquier, F. & Rapoport, H. Globalization, Brain Drain and Development. Bonn: Institute for the Study of Labor (IZA)

Easterly, W. (2006, November 27). Aid Effectiveness: A Debate Between Steve Radelet and William Easterly. Center for Global Development. Retrieved from https://www.cgdev.org/blog/aid-effectiveness-debate-between-steve-radelet-and-william-easterly

Easterly, W. (2013). *The Tyranny of Experts*. New York: Basic Books.

Economy into Worst Recession since World War II". Retrieved from:

https://www.worldbank.org/en/news/press-release/2020/06/08/covid-19-to-plunge-global-economy-into-worst-recession-since-world-war-ii.print.

European Anti-Poverty Network (EAPN). "Facts & Trends." Retrieved from: https://www.eapn.eu/what-is –poverty/poverty-facts-and-trends/.

Exodus of Talent" in *Inside Higher Ed*. Retrieved from https://www.insidehighered.com/print/blogs/world-view/medical-education-and-ethiopian-exodus-talent

Failing and What Can Be Done About It. New York: Oxford University Press.

FAO (2001). (Protecting Small Farmers and the Rural Poor in the

Forbes. "World's Billionaires List: The Richest in 2020". Retrieved from https://www.forbes.com/billionaires

From https://unctad.org/en/pages/PublicationWebflyer.aspx?publicationid=2571

Fullbrook, E. (Ed.) (2007). *Real-World Economics: A Post-Autistic Economics Reader.* New York: Anthem Press.

Germain, JC. (2020). *The Impact of Corruption on Growth and Development.* Columbia, SC: KDP Publishing.

Goldberg, P.K. (2007) & Pavcknik, N. (2007). "Distributional Effects of Globalization in Developing Countries." *Journal of Economic Literature* Vol. XLV (March 2007) pp.39-82.

Government of Maldives (2009). Impacts of Graduation from Least Developed Countries. Retrieved from http://www.maldivespartnershipforum.gov,mv./pdf/impacts%20of%0ldc%20graduation.pdf

Graduation from group of LDCs. Retrieved from http://www.unohrlis.org/en/un-envoy-hails-cape-verde-graduation-frm-group-ldcs.

Hall, J.C., Karadas, S., & Schlosky, M.T.T. (2016, December 15). Is There Moral Hazard in the Heavily Indebted Poor Countries (HIPC) Initiative Debt Relief Process? Retrieved from http://business.wvu.edu/graduate-degrees/phd-economics/working-papers.

https://oxfam.org/en/press-releases/words-billionaires-have-more-wealth-46-billion-people.

https://www.wider.unu.edu/publication/aid-and-poverty-reduction .

https://www.wto.org.english/news_e/news20_e/devel_11nov-e.

IMF (2001, August 2). Debt Relief for Poverty Reduction: The Role of the Enhanced HIPC Initiative. Retrieved from https://www.imf.org/external/pubs/ftexrp/debt/eng

IMF (2008, July). Liberia: Poverty Reduction Strategy Paper. IMF Country Report No. 08/2019.

IMF (2020, March 25). Debt Relief Under the Indebted Poor Country (HIPC) Initiative. Retrieved from https://www.imf.org/en/About/Factsheets/Sheets/2016/08/01/

Inequality.org. (2015, February). "Eight Ways to Reduce Global Inequality." Retrieved from www.inequality.org/great-divide/8-ways-reduce-global-inequality/

Inequality.org. (2020, August). "Twelve U.S. Billionaires Have a   Combined $1 Trillion". Retrieved from www.inequality.org/great/divide/twelve-us-https://inequality.org/facts/inequalitybillionaires-combined-1-trillion/.

Inequality.org. "Covid-19 and Inequality". Retrieved from: https://inequality.org/facts/inequality-and-covid-19/.

Isar, S. (2012). Was the Highly Indebted Poor Country Initiative (HIPC) a Success? *The Journal of Sustainable Development* (Vol.9. Issue I, pp.107-122).

Lessons from Latin American HIPCs (Working Paper 262). London: Overseas Development Institute.

Milanovic, B., Reddy, S. & Polaski, S. (2006, January 27). Why Have the Poorest Countries Failed to Develop? Washington, DC: Carnegie Endowment for International Peace. Retrieved from http://www.carnegieendowment.org//2006/01/27-why-have-the-poorest-countries-failed-to-develop-event-847.

MPI (2013, September). The Impact of Remittances on Economic Growth and Poverty Reduction. *Policy Brief* No 8. Retrieved from www.migrationpolicy.org

ODI (2006, February).Politics and Poverty Reduction Strategies:

OXFAM International (2020, January 20). "World billionaires have more wealth than 4.6 billion people". Retrieved from

Piketty. T. (2014). *Capital in the Twenty-First Century*. Cambridge, MA: The Belknap Press of Harvard University Press.

Reiter, J. & Adhikari, R. (2016). 4 Ways the world's least developed countries can improve trade.

World Economic Forum. Retrieved from
https://www.weforum.org/agenda/2016/05/4-
ways-the-least-developed-countries-can-improve-
trade/

Retrieved from:
https//www.un.org/development/desa/dspd/w
p-
content/uploads/sites/22/2018/09/McKnight2.
pdf.

Rose-Ackerman, S. & Palifka, B. J. (2016). *Corruption and Government:*

Roser, M. & Ortiz-Ospina, E. (2013). "Global Extreme Poverty." Retrieved from:
https://ourworldindata.org/extreme-poverty.

Sachs, J.D. (2005). *The End of Poverty.* New York: The Penguin Press.

Tamrat, W. (2019, July 15). "Medical Education and the Ethiopian

The Economist (2020). "Inequality in India." *The Economist* (December 5th-11th).

The Economist (2020). "The dismal yet flexible science: When the facts change." *The Economist* (August 8th-14th).

The Economist (2020). "The World This Year." *The Economist* (December 19th, 2020 – January 1st, 2021).

Therichest.com. "What Billionaires Do With Their Money?" Retrieved from https://www.therichest.com/world/what-billionaires-do-with-their-money/#:~:text=What-Billionaires Do-With-heir Money%3F- 1-Come, Education. 5 Phi…

UNCTAD (2001, May 14-20). Country presentation by The Government of Maldives. Retrieved from http://www.unctad.org/searchcenter/pages/results.aspx?k=maldives.

UNCTAD (2016). *The Least Developed Countries Report 2016*. New York: United Nations Publications.

UNCTAD (2017). *The Least Developed Countries Report 2017*. New York: United Nations Publications.

UNCTAD (2019). *The Least Developed Countries Report 2019*. Retrieved

UNCTAD (2020, November 12). COVID-19 and beyond: What role for LDCs? Retrieved from https://unctad.org/news/covid-19-and-beyond-what-role-ldcs.

UNEP. "Food and food waste." Retrieved from https//www.unenvironment.org/explore-topics/resource-efficiency/what-we-do/sustainable-lifestyles/food-and-food-waste

UNFPA (2017, 20 July). What is Family Planning? Retrieved from https://www.unfpa.org/family-planning

UNIRSD (2010). *Combating Poverty and Inequality: Structural Change, Social Policy, and Politics.* France: UNIRSD Publication.

United Nations (2008, February 19). UN envoy hails Cape Verde

United Nations. "Ending Poverty." Retrieved from https://www.un.org/en/sections/issues-depth/poverty

UNU-WIDER (2005). Aid and Poverty Reduction. Retrieved from

USDA. "Food Waste FAQs." Retrieved from: https://www.usda.gov/foodwaste/faqs

Washington, DC: World Bank.

Weil, D. N. (2016). *Economic Growth.* New York: Routledge

WIR 2018. World Inequality Report 2018. Retrieved from https://wir2018.wid.world/part-2.html.

World Bank (2001, September 6-8). Economic Development vs Social Exclusion: The Cost of Development in Brazil. Washington, D.C. World Bank.

World Bank (2007). Evaluation of Poverty Reduction Support Credits:

World Bank (2014, 23 June). "Theorist Eric Maskin: Globalization Is Increasing Inequality." Retrieved from https://www.worldbank.org/en/news/feature/2

014/06/23/theorist-eric-maskin-globalization-is-increasing-inequality.print

World Bank (2016). *World Development Indicators 2016.*

World Bank (2018, January 11). Heavily Indebted Poor Country (HIPC) Initiative. Retrieved from: https://www.worldbank.org/topic/debt/hipc

World Bank (2020, 16 April). "Understanding Poverty." Retrieved from https://www.worldbank.org/en/topic/poverty/overview

World Bank (2020, 7 January). "Countdown to 2030: A Race against time to end extreme poverty". Retrieved from https://blogs.worldbank.org/voices/countdown-2030-race-against-time-end-poverty?cid=ECR_E_NewsletterWeekly_EN_EXT&deliveryName=...

World Bank (2020, 8 June). "Press Release: COVID-19 to Plunge Global

World Economic Forum (WEF, January 20). "3 charts that explain global inequality". Retrieved from https://www.weforum.org/agenda/2016/01/3-charts-that-explain-global-inequality.

World Health Organization (WHO). "Social determinants of health – Social exclusion." Retrieved from https://www.who.int/social_determinats/themes/socialexclusion

WTO (2020, November 11). The least developed countries were hit hard by the trade downturn triggered by the COVID-19 pandemic. Retrieved from https://www.wto.org.english/news_e/news20_e/devel_11nov-e.

Made in the USA
Columbia, SC
24 August 2021

43286001R00111